Journeys of a Boomer

Sojourns, Sorrows and Sunshine in the Life of a Baby Boomer

Holly Richardson

DEDICATION

For Ginger and Kristy, Jim and Martin, who are my lifelines

For Peyton, Scott, Charlotte, Brendan and Cameron, who give my life meaning

And for Eric, who saved it

TABLE OF CONTENTS

JOURNEYS OF A BOOMER

ACKNOWLEDGMENTS

This book would not have been possible without the help and support of so many of my friends. My heartfelt appreciation to you all.

To **Johannes Tysee**, for the cover photo. For me it captures the essence of what I was trying to write about: sailing through life, sometimes into the clouds, sometimes into the sunshine. I am grateful you are the Captain of my favorite ship and more importantly, my friend.

To **Joe Bonsall**, for the Foreword, and for being my friend for over thirty-five years. We've been through a lot together, and I know you are always in my corner.

To **Mary Wallace** and **Joan Conley**, who plodded through an unedited version of this book, and saved my creditability with their edits.

And for moral support and encouragement:

To my **Family**, for the inspiration, and the love and the strength you have given me.

To **Mindy Benson**, my sister from another mother. Thanks for the texts, phone calls and always believing in me, even when I didn't believe in myself.

To **Candy**, who started me on my road to recovery by being my roommate in Norway. Even through the tears, we did have fun!

To **Claudia**, my longtime bestie. How lucky I am to always be able to count on you for anything.

To **Diana Maloziec**, for being my biggest cheerleader.

And to **Mark Hunt**, my forever friend. He knows why.

FOREWORD

I am a Baby Boomer just like your author Holly Richardson. I have in fact just turned seventy and like Holly I am just not certain where all the time has gone. The Book of James tells us that our lives are a vapor that passes quickly, and I can attest to the fact that my vapor has moved right on along. But as the old Gospel song so beautifully illustrates, "I Wouldn't Take Nothing for My Journey Now."

I am certain your author feels the same. I am of course an optimistic person, a glass half full sort of guy, although I enjoy a sunset as much as I do a sunrise. Yes, there is as much sadness as there is joy and much defeat before certain victories for each one of us. Each chapter in this book reveals every side of growing and learning and dealing with pitfalls as well as blessings through decades of times passing; and I believe every reader, whether a boomer or not can identify with Holly.

I have known Holly since 1982 as illustrated in Chapter Nine. I call it "The Oak Ridge Boys Chapter," and we are all honored to be included in this book. But if I might get even more personal, on Holly's trip to Normandy, which is also chronicled in these pages, it was my father who she was honoring. When I decided in 2003 to write a book about my own parents it was Holly who helped me get it right. I wrote a chapter every day and would send it to Holly every night and she would respond with edits and ideas. My book G I Joe and Lillie would not exist without Holly Richardson and I will be forever grateful. I hope to also visit the Normandy beaches one day where my father landed as a young, nineteen year old soldier in the first wave on that Day of Days.

Thank you again Holly for remembering him in this memoir. I am also grateful that she asked me to write a few words here. Her story is filled with love and humor and heartaches just like your story...and mine.

Without giving anything away I know that some of the things in this book were very hard to write about. I feel that Holly may have regained a portion of needed strength by writing of the sadder events in her life, but I'll tell you I also found strength by reading them.

I might add that her lessons-learned guidebook is an important read for all of us. The voyeur inside of us loves to peek though someone else's window and Holly has opened her heart here and let us have a solid glimpse into one baby boomer's life that in so many ways becomes a looking glass experience for most of us.

Thank you Holly for writing about your journey. As a fellow baby boomer, I felt every page. And by the way, I also once owned a Davy Crockett coonskin cap and it will come as no surprise to Holly that her baseball stories were my favorites! Read on...

Joe Bonsall / 45 year member of the American Music Group **The Oak Ridge Boys** and author of ten books

PROLOGUE: SUNRISE OR SUNSET?

May every sunrise hold more promise, and every sunset hold more peace.

I t's hard to tell if this photo is a sunrise or sunset, isn't it? Actually, it was taken in Norway on a beautiful late June evening, sometime just around midnight. So it is neither, or both. In the Land of the Midnight Sun, the sun never actually sets before it starts to rise again.

As a card-carrying member of the Baby Boomer generation, I have found that life brings its own unique set of joys and sorrows. Oftentimes, you find yourself reminiscing about an idyllic childhood in a time and place far removed from today's reality.

Other times you are grateful for being able to reap the rewards of a life well lived, coasting along, enjoying the special privileges that come with aging: grandchildren, financial security, travel and freedom from the stresses of earlier years.

But if the unthinkable happens - the unexpected and sudden death of a spouse - and you find yourself in the eye of a hurricane where life may go on calmly around you, but you are in the midst of a Category 5, how do you cope? How do you reflect on the past...and the future? How do you handle the shock and the immediate aftermath? What do you do about a drastic and sudden loss of income? How do you deal with changes in relationships with friends and family? Most importantly, where do you find joy and how?

This book looks back at the experiences of my life growing up in the fifties and sixties, married life and young parenthood in the seventies and beyond, and then navigating through the challenges of sudden widowhood. Sometimes humorous, sometimes poignant, I hope some of my stories will strike a cord with you.

1 BEGINNING JOURNEY/FATHER KNOWS BEST

Childhood is freedom.

Indian Proverb

Left to right: My father Bob Anderson, me, paternal grandparents Elmer and Jeanette Anderson, sister Dawn, maternal grandfather Walter Stecher, my mother Marian Anderson, maternal grandmother Ann Stecher, at a family picnic, 1958

The Anderson family of Maple Street in Springfield, Illinois, was the quintessential American family of the 1950's. Coming into our living rooms every week for nine years via the television screen, they were supposed to represent reality. Father Jim (Robert Young) came home every night after working at his insurance agency. Waiting for him were his wife, Margaret (Jane Wyatt), and children, Betty (Elinor Donahue), Bud (Billy Gray) and Kathy (Lauren Chapin). Jim would exchange his sport coat for a sweater as Margaret appeared from the kitchen (it was always the kitchen), and the kids bounded down the stairs to greet him. Wise and calm, he was able to soothe over whatever problems had occurred that day.

Actually, the series title was more figurative than literal, for Father didn't always know best. Jim Anderson not only lost his temper from time to time, but was occasionally wrong as well. Although Margaret was stuck in the drudgery of domestic servitude, she was nobody's fool, often besting her husband and son. Daughter Betty (known affectionately to her father as Princess) could also take the male Andersons to task, as could the precocious Kathy (nicknamed Kitten), the baby of the family. However, they all seemed to love one another, work through their problems and live their lives in relative tranquility. They came into our living rooms from 1954 through 1960, gently preached moral issues, won several Emmys, and when the cast decided to call it quits, still ranked sixth in the Neilson ratings. Many critics viewed the series at best as campy, at worst as utterly unrepresentative of what life in the 1950's was like.

Our family would have disagreed however, for we were The

Andersons, literally and figuratively. I was eight when the show first premiered, and it immediately became my favorite. Exactly my age, little Kathy dressed in jeans and plaid shirts, or smocked dresses with Peter Pan collars, sported freckles and wore her hair in pigtails. I thought I looked just like her, but for the hair color. I longed for a dreamy big brother like Bud, and aspired one day to be attractive and sophisticated like Betty. There were some discrepancies between their screen life and my actual one, but they were minor and in my mind, inconsequential. In real life, I had a little sister who was not represented in the cast, my dad sold real estate rather than insurance, and although my mom seemed to spend a lot of time in the kitchen, just like Margaret, she vacuumed in pants, NOT a shirtwaist dress and pearls. To me, the show *was* my life, with its little trials and tribulations, always fixable by the love of two parents. The fictional characters lived on Maple Street in Springfield, somewhere in the Midwest. We lived on Hamlin Avenue in Park Ridge, Illinois. However, there was a town named Springfield in Illinois, so I figured that was close enough. To cement the relationship between television make believe and reality, our last name was indeed Anderson.

Park Ridge is located fifteen miles northwest of Chicago, and in the decade of 1950-1960 its population doubled from about sixteen thousand to thirty-two thousand. Our family added three souls to this population explosion when we moved into a small ranch house there in 1953, and one more when my baby sister, Dawn, was born in 1954.

The town was white, waspish, and a postcard for middle-America. I cannot remember one of my friend's mothers who worked. All of the dads came home around 6 pm to a hot dinner. The boys played Little League; the girls played house. Almost everybody had a dog, a back yard and a swing set. Our pediatrician, Dr. Cant, could, and did, make house calls. We had barbecues with our grandparents or the neighbors on the weekends; we went to church on Sunday. Our parents were active in the PTA or Brownies or Cub Scouts or all three.

Besides "Father Knows Best," my favorite TV shows were "Mickey Mouse Club" (particularly Spin and Marty episodes, or anything with Annette Funicello in it), "Superman," "Captain Kangaroo," "The Howdy Doody Show," "The Lone Ranger," and "Davy Crockett, King of the Wild Frontier." It was mandatory to don your coonskin cap while watching ol' Davy. Was there a child in America that did not own one? My parents favored "I Love Lucy," "Perry Como," "Sgt. Bilko," and "Dragnet." There was an issue, however, with "Dragnet" in our house. My parents loved it, and so did I. Set in Los Angeles, it was a cop show, which chronicled actual L.A. Police Department cases in a fictionalized form. Jack Webb played Sergeant Joe Friday, the quiet, dark-haired, jug-eared hero who introduced each episode with the case crime of the week, and the introductory line, "My name's Friday." The only problem was that Mom and Dad thought it was too violent for me to watch, so they banned me to my bedroom to play records or read. It was their version of parental censorship. Many a Thursday night I would sit cross-legged just outside my bedroom door, blocked from seeing the small television set by a wall. However, from this vantage point, I was at least able to hear the dialogue. I never found out if I was actually pulling one over on Mom or Dad or not, but I thought I was being clever.

We played with Hula Hoops, Silly Putty and Mr. Potato Head. In those days, Mr. Potato Head did not come with a plastic potato; we had to use a real one. To express our creativity, we would

4

paint masterpieces by number. The canvas came as an outline, with every space color-coded. The fancier versions of these sets had real oil based paints. I think I painted a hundred of them. In fact, as a throwback to childhood, my future husband and I painted one together during our engagement. It was a better way to occupy our time, my mother thought, than "necking" on the couch! It seems parental values were still being subtly practiced.

We listened to a young man named Elvis Presley on our record players. Except me. I was never a big Elvis fan, although I am not sure why. My mother was not especially fond of the way he wiggled his hips, so perhaps there was another form of censorship taking place. I do remember that I much preferred Perry Como. I owned all his albums and listened to him by the hour. I remember the heartbreak when my sister sat on my recording of "Hot Diggity, Dog Ziggity, Boom What You Do to Me." I had saved up for that precious 45 with my babysitting money, and life as I knew it would not be the same until it was replaced.

The best form of entertainment for me, however, was baseball. My dad often took me to legendary Wrigley Field, even as a little girl. At least once a year, it was always our special day together. Mom loathed baseball, but she packed us a lunch, which we promptly discarded once we got to the park, in favor of peanuts, crackerjack, hot dogs, pizza and/or Frosty Malts. Back in those days, the Cubs were only ten years or so removed from their last World Series appearance, so hope was still a viable commodity. My favorite player was Ernie Banks, but mostly I just loved being at the ballpark. I loved the smell of the hot dogs and beer and freshly cut grass. I loved the crack of a bat driving a ball into the outfield, or the smack of a ball in a glove, or the roar of the crowd. I still do. Baseball marked some of the best times of my childhood, and to me it is still one of life's simple pleasures.

Every night we would all eat dinner together in a little kitchen off the living room. There was no TV in that room to distract us, no late night school activities, no working late. Dad came home at a specific time, and dinner was usually on the table within half an hour. When my parents went out for an evening, they hired a babysitter, and we all got a special treat. It was a little aluminum tray, divided into three sections. The sections held frozen chicken, corn, and mashed potatoes. After only about half an hour in the oven, out popped a hot, cooked meal. Swanson's TV dinners were one of the wonderful inventions of the 1950's.

On rare occasions, we went out for dinner. In Des Plaines, the next town over, a little restaurant sold hamburgers for 15 cents, as well as French fries and milk shakes. In addition, it was all ready to eat in just a few seconds. In fact, my Dad met a man one day who asked him to invest in this restaurant. He said he was going to build a lot more of them, and he gave my Dad an opportunity to get in at the ground floor. However, his $3,000 asking price seemed a little steep to a man with two young children and a mortgage, so Dad turned him down. The man was Ray Kroc, and the little restaurant was McDonald's.

While Elvis or Perry were on the record player, while the Cubs continued losing, while we went to work and to school and played with hula hoops, and while "Father Knows Best" came into our living rooms, the world was changing around us. Racial tensions were high, and Rosa Parks refused to sit in the back of the bus. A little girl in Topeka, Kansas, learned that the Supreme Court determined that she no longer had to cross railroad tracks and a busy street to go to a black school, but instead could attend the much closer all white school. Despite the decision, resistance to its implementation was strong, particularly in the south.

At the same time, a frightening awareness of the world's new weapons, brought about by the 1945 detonation of the atomic bomb in Japan, increased fear of the Soviet Union and the spread of communism. The Cold War began in earnest, and was to be an underlying threat for decades. Nikita Khrushchev said he would bury us, and the Russians beat us into space. Fearful of the apparent superiority of Soviet technology and the specter of nuclear war, many Americans built bomb shelters in their backyards. Schools held bombing drills along with fire drills. In my innocence, I believed that covering my head and hiding under my metal and wooden desk would protect me from all terror. The television programming of the day did not portray these problems, and despite all the foreboding, my life was protected, safe, secure and idyllic. The 1950's were a terrific time to grow up and be an innocent child. It was a time to grow, play, and learn. It was a time when no one worried too much about tomorrow. Everything would work out somehow. After all, Father Knew Best.

2 HISTORICAL JOURNEY/NOVEMBER 21, 1963

*And so, my fellow Americans: ask not what your country can do for you
—ask what you can do for your country.*

John F. Kennedy

E ven though the tranquility of the fifties had undercurrents of
unrest, it was not really until one particular November day
that all vestiges of innocence came to a shattering end. Early
that particular afternoon, I was in my sophomore geometry
class at Maine East High School, unsuccessfully trying to
figure out trapezoids and parallelograms, and wondering why I
needed this information in my head at all. My teacher had the
unusual name of Ronnoc Connor. Ronnoc was Connor spelled
backwards. I thought that nugget of information was much more
curious and interesting than the subject he taught. Suddenly, an
office worker rushed into the classroom and asked to see me.
Since I was a good student and one of those boring kids that never
got into trouble, I was startled.

"You need to go to the radio station right away," she informed me.

This too was odd. I was a part time announcer at the small FM station that broadcast from the campus. I think it had a listening area of about one hundred yards surrounding the school, but it was good practice for those of us who fancied ourselves future broadcasters. Upon entering the closet-like space that served as a studio, I was greeted by the radio station director, also a teacher.

"There has been a shooting," he solemnly told me. "The President has been wounded in Dallas."

We turned to the national broadcast on the Chicago AM station and listened together. Within moments, it was confirmed that the President had not only been shot, but had been killed.

"You are the announcer today," he said, his voice sounding strange and far away. "You need to go on the air and broadcast the news to the students."

A flip of a switch piped the radio station into all the classrooms, which I suppose made it more or less like an intercom system. By this time, the principal had also arrived and the little closet was getting warm and claustrophobic.

"The district is dismissing all students at the end of this period," he informed me. "After you are done with the bulletin, introduce me and I will come on the air and make that announcement."

I followed instructions, although I have no recollection of what I actually said. I imagine it was probably a word-for-word rehash of what we had heard on the national news broadcast. Cocooned in the tiny studio, I could only imagine the gasps of horror and looks of shock on the faces of my classmates throughout the various rooms. Several minutes later, the hallways were completely silent, even as two thousand students moved through them. It was like watching a silent movie; kids opened their lockers, removed what they needed, made their way to the exits, no one speaking a syllable. I walked from the bus stop with my friend Nancy Reinhardt. We both went inside her home, and found her mother watching television. Watching is perhaps not the right word. Staring transfixed would better describe it. Mrs. Reinhardt, one of my mother's good friends, simply looked up at us with swollen eyes, and barely whispered, "Holly, you better go right home. Your mother would want you there."

So I walked the additional two blocks and entered my own house, only to find the same scene repeated. There was my mother, the rock of our household, looking just like Mrs. Reinhardt: eyes swollen and red, welling with tears, fixated on the black and white images on the screen in front of her. There was the incredible sight of the young Mrs. Kennedy, her suit swathed with dark stains that could only be blood, climbing aboard a plane, following the casket bearing the body of the President of the United States.

The days to follow brought their own indelible images, many burned in our memories forever. There was the oath of office to the new President aboard Air Force One, the salute from a young son, the rider-less horse, the eternal flame. However, another image that I will always retain is that of my strong and resolute mother, a Republican to her core, with tears staining her cheeks as the young Democratic President was gunned down. The innocence of the 1950's was officially over for me, for it was the first day I saw my mother cry. Little did I know that innocence would be shattered again thirty-eight years later on a beautiful September morning in New York, Washington, D.C. and Pennsylvania.

3 LEGACY JOURNEY/MR. SCHNABLE

A wise teacher makes learning a joy.

Proverb

Wayne Schnable's British History class. Author far right.

H is face was pock-marked, he was overweight, and sported a crew-cut. He had a booming voice that resonated throughout a building. He did not hesitate to use it if he thought it would be effective, and it usually succeeded in getting everyone's attention. He also was witty and intelligent, and I loved him. His full name was Wayne David Schnable, and he was my high school history teacher.

When I was a teenager my parents moved from the little square house in which I had spent virtually my entire life to a large home on a lake surrounding a golf course. Although it was only half an hour north of the old place, this new home might as well have been on the moon. I was in a new school with strange faces. And I was sixteen. Mr. Schnable was my teacher for first period on that first day at my new high school, Ela-Vernon in Lake Zurich, Illinois. It was a small school at that time, only a few hundred students in all four grades, so everybody knew everybody else. Except for me, of course. I don't remember much about that day except that he made me laugh. I was introduced as the "new kid," but in a kind way. He helped break the ice for me and soon I started making new friends.

I also loved his class. American History was a requirement for juniors in high school, and he made it come alive. He challenged us; he put us right into whatever period of history we were studying. He encouraged our interaction, and he encouraged us to be his friend. Now in my teenage exuberance, I think I might have taken this invitation a little too far, when on April Fools Day I stole his coat from his office and hid it in a classroom. He was NOT amused.

My senior year a new school was built to accommodate our expanding district, and because of where our home was located, I was to attend my third high school in four years. The transition was made easier, however, when I discovered that Mr. Schnable would be transferring to the new school as well. The school offered a unique opportunity; there were to be enrichment classes held after school in a variety of subjects for any students interested. I immediately signed up for British History when I discovered Mr. Schnable would be the teacher. There were four students in the class: Richard Pearson, June Tinker, Sandy Wilewski and me.

What fun we had! Some people might think British History interesting; some might think it staid and boring. I thought it was hilarious! We would sometimes have the entire two-hour class taught in the worst British accent you can imagine. The Battle of Hastings was fought by our fearless leader running from one side of the classroom to the other, alternating portrayals of Harold II of England and Duke William of Normandy. Tests were referred to as "Fun and Games, Kiddies," and that's just what it was for the four of us. We all aced the class, because we all enjoyed it so much.

High school graduation eventually loomed, and that meant of course, leaving high school. I was off to Cornell College in Iowa, and although I looked forward to the adventure ahead, I truly wished Mr. Schnable would decide to become a college professor and uproot his family to the cornfields. Such was not to be. But he did keep in touch with me. He wrote me long, philosophical letters, and told me that since I was now an adult, I should call him Wayne. I never was able to do that. I did write to him about my triumphs and tragedies, as only an emotional nineteen-year-old can do. He would always respond promptly, with encouragement and advice.

After a couple of years, I stopped hearing from him. I didn't think too much of it, as I was busy on campus and working on my studies.   At home for the summer before my senior year, the news that he had died hit me like a sledgehammer. Cancer had taken him quickly. He was only in his forties and he left a wife and two young boys behind.

But he also left behind quite a legacy. I still remember him as one of the great influences of my young life. I know I am not alone. Every young person should have a Mr. Schnable in their lives. I'm so grateful for mine.

4 AWAKENNG JOURNEY/FROM BEANIES TO BIAS, THE COLLEGE YEARS

I have never let my schooling interfere with my education.

Mark Twain

King Chapel, on the campus of Cornell College, Mt. Vernon, Iowa

Driving west on Interstate 30 From Illinois, we could see the spires and turrets long before we approached the town of

Mt. Vernon, Iowa. King Chapel stood tall and proud like a beacon in this small mid-western town, a majestic stone edifice incongruously surrounded by cornfields. It was here that I was about to make my home for four years.

In the autumn of 1966, like decades of autumns before and after, the maple and oak trees that dotted the campus painted it in swaths of scarlet, russet and amber. The red brick buildings and quiet streets whispered of the quintessential campus life that was about to greet me. After depositing me in the two-story Pfeiffer Hall dorm, named after a college mega-buck benefactor, my parents left me to my new life. The first order of business was to be outfitted, for I needed to pick up my beanie. A freshman ritual, all members of our lowly class were to wear purple beanies on our heads for six weeks, emblazoned with the year of our graduation: 1970. My, but 1970 seemed so far away that first uncertain day. There exists a photo of this humiliation in my yearbook; scores of freshman ladies in a circle with their index fingers perched on the button of the beanie, obviously singing and dancing to some song. Upper class women stood on a knoll directing the performance. We had it easy, however. The freshman men, also known as Monks, were required to dance around the campus in various contorted poses, also sporting their telltale beanies. They could often be seen in Congo type lines, hands to ankles, walking backwards or doing the elephant walk. For whatever reason, this behavior provided entertainment for decades of upperclassmen at Cornell. Today, it would probably be considered harassment or hazing; in the turbulent sixties, it was frivolity. We also amused ourselves with pie eating contests, Winter Festivals, painting the Rock (a huge boulder that held untold thousands of layers of graffiti from various groups), picnicking at nearby Palisades Park, and philanthropic activities.

There was a group at school called the Campus Chest, which raised money for various worthwhile local or national charities. Each year male and female students were elected Mr. and Miss Campus Chest. At all of the club's activities, they would each wear a sweatshirt proclaiming their title. Fine for the guy, I suppose, but just visualize a 1968 co-ed with Miss Campus Chest plastered all over her...um...chest. To my knowledge, for the four years I was at Cornell, NO ONE ever questioned this practice.

Cornell was and is a private institution. By the time I graduated, tuition had topped $3,000, which was a king's ransom in those days. There also were not the scholarship opportunities that there are today. How my parents scraped together the money each year so I could attend this school, I will never know. Some of the steep tuition money went to bringing an impressive list of performers and artists to campus to share their talents. All performances or celebrity lecturers held court in King Chapel, and those walls held the likes of the New Christy Minstrels, Judy Collins, Peter Nero, the Houston Symphony with conductor Andre Previn, Max Neuhaus, John Denver, Julian Bond, Josh White and Aaron Copland, to name a few.

Academics were not forgotten by any means. Cornell had the reputation (and still does) of being one of the top-notch private small colleges in the Midwest. The faculty was composed of scores of men and women who were truly innovators and scholars in their various fields. Classes were small and individualized; there were no huge meeting halls at this school.

It was a beautiful place to spend four years, with friendly people, great educators, good old-fashioned fun and celebrity visitors dropping in to perform. However, to this day, I have never sent a nickel to my alma mater, and have attended only one reunion. My time there was forever tainted by two episodes, episodes that although they were separate, in my mind were always intertwined. Both were results of the times, but they influenced my thought processes from that moment on.

On October 17, 1968, a group of black students entered Old Sem, the administration building, and demanded certain rights. Among them were more classes focusing on black issues and preferential treatment in selection processes for special programs. The administration took a hard stand, and called the authorities. The day ended without violence or incident and the students were removed from the building. However, I was stunned when I watched the news coverage that night. All the Iowa television stations reported the "uprising" at Cornell, and showed images of police in battle gear confronting shouting students. It was a complete misrepresentation of what actually occurred, as most of the campus population was most decidedly NOT on the side of the protestors. Cornell was a Methodist-affiliated campus with a mostly white student body from the middle to upper middle class. Although many were against the war in Vietnam, civil disobedience and protesting were just not part of our makeup. Arguments could certainly be made that when it came to social injustices we were all living in a fantasy world. Nevertheless, it was our world at the time. Blacks on campus were few in number, and most of them were not particularly militant either. It simply was a story about a few students who broke into a building to make a point. However, that was not how the media portrayed the incident. It was an interesting lesson in journalism, and it colored my view of the profession. From that day forward, I have always wondered if a story I read in the paper is accurate. It was perhaps the genesis of the "fake journalism" we often see today. My eldest daughter has been a journalist for over two decades now, and she might take issue with that statement. I will agree that this is a gray area to be sure. For me, however, I witnessed media exaggeration first hand, and have not ever forgotten it.

The second event was directly related to the first and affected me personally. I had turned down a modest monetary award from the State of Illinois that if accepted, required me to go to an Illinois institution. I turned it down because I wanted to go to Cornell College in Iowa. Cornell had enticed me with their Semester in Washington program, which was a chance to spend one semester at American University studying politics. Four months living and studying in our nation's capital was a dream that I had nurtured since my early years in high school. Only four people were chosen each year and the selection process was based primarily on academic standing. When the winners were announced, I was devastated to learn that I had placed fifth, even though my class rank placed me fourth among the applicants. The young man chosen in my place, the one who was not as qualified according to the application requirements, was a Black man, one of the ones who had taken over the administration building a few months before. The selection committee had indeed buckled to the demands made by a few vociferous students; they just had not done it the day of the incident. Today this is known as affirmative action, and I experienced it up close and personal. My father, an attorney and a reasonable man, drove from our Chicago area home to Mt. Vernon to plead my case. It was to no avail; their minds were made up. Even though I felt I had earned it, my dream was not to be, and I did not get to participate in the Washington Semester. Six semesters into my college education, it was too late to transfer schools, so I stayed, graduated, and moved back to Illinois with a tainted view of my alma mater.

Every year since then I have received solicitations in the mail from Cornell, asking me to make an alumni donation. Every year they are tossed. However, these incidents, painful as they were, also helped form one of my core beliefs. I am firmly opposed to affirmative action: I believe that people should be judged on their merits, regardless of race, creed or religion. If a person is the best-qualified person for a job, or elected office or any other position, the choice should be made based on their qualifications. Period. Not whether they are black, white or purple. Not whether they are male or female. Not whether they are gay or straight. I am grateful to Cornell for defining that for me; just not grateful enough to ever give them money.

Graduation photo, 1970

5 HISTORICAL JOURNEY/VIETNAM

War is wretched beyond description, and only a fool or a fraud could

sentimentalize its cruel reality

Sen. John McCain

Vietnam Memorial, Washington, DC

No Baby Boomer memoir would be complete without some mention of Vietnam and the war that consumed our nation between the mid 1960's and mid 1970's. I was lucky in that I was not touched personally by the war. Rather than the all-volunteer armed forces like we have today, a lottery was established in 1969 to determine the order in which young men would be called to serve. The draft itself was an interesting spectacle. All men born between January 1, 1944 and December 31, 1950 were eligible that first year. Birthdates were assigned a number, 1 through 366 (including February 29), printed on a piece of paper, encased in a capsule, mixed in a shoebox and placed in a glass jar. All capsules were then drawn one by one. The first one drawn was 258 or September 14th. All men born on that date were assigned number one. The first 195 birthdates drawn were later called to serve in the order they were chosen.

Just because I had no relatives that served did not mean I was immune to what was going on around me. The Vietnam War was the first American war that came into our living rooms every night via the news in all its bloody glory. It became very unpopular very quickly and protests abounded throughout the nation, one larger than the next. It also escalated quickly and more and more of our brothers, cousins and friends were dying on a daily basis, all documented in living color. It divided our nation, not for the first time, but perhaps forever. When the boys that survived did come home, they were met with at best indifference, at worst hostility. It was such a change from the celebrations of a short generation before when World War II ended. It seemed everyone just wanted to forget about this stain on our history. The only people that couldn't forget it of course were those that were there, and the families of those who never came home.

Many years later, my husband and I were in Washington D.C., with another couple and it was a priority for our friend Jack to visit the Vietnam Wall. Erected in 1982, its two black granite walls forming a "V" and etched with over 58,000 names of those who died in the conflict is an iconic memorial in the nation's capitol. Jack served in the Army in Vietnam for two years and saw heavy action. He was 6 foot 4 inches tall, weighed north of 200 pounds and was an imposing figure. But as he walked the length of the memorial, my husband by his side, he started shaking with emotion and sobbing like a baby. He had buddies on that wall, and for many moments was inconsolable. The war became real for me that day.

Many years after that, I had the opportunity to visit the former South Vietnam, specifically Ho Chi Minh City, which was formerly known as Saigon. I saw the building where the children were airlifted from near the U.S. Embassy as our troops were withdrawing in defeat; I visited the War Remembrance Museum, where the American atrocities are magnified and the Vietnamese cruelties never mentioned; I interacted with the citizens of a now unified Vietnam, curious about Americans they have only heard stories about. It was a fascinating cultural experience, but all I could think about was how lucky I was to be able to observe it all without an ever present ache in my soul, because I had been an observer, and had not lost someone I loved.

6 LOVE JOURNEY/YELLOW ROSES

They do not love who do not show their love.

William Shakespeare

Our wedding day, June 17, 1972

E very year for decades on our anniversary, my husband brought me yellow roses. In the early years, I received one for each year we were married. As the years accumulated and the price of roses soared, he perhaps would settle for an even dozen. Sometimes an expensive florist delivered them, sometimes Scott would stop at a grocery store on the way home. One year when finances were particularly tight, he picked one from the back yard.

We met at DePaul University Law School, which both of us entered directly after graduation from college. He was a Chicago city boy, born and raised, and had attended DePaul University for undergraduate school. I was raised in the suburbs and went to a rural college. But on the first day of law school, we found ourselves sitting right behind each other in Richard Groll's Properties class. I was at a distinct advantage that first day of law school. There were only three women in our entire first year class, for in 1970 not many women were yet choosing law as a career. I'm not exactly sure why I was either. My father had changed careers from real estate to law school, becoming an attorney in the early 1960's. I was also interested in politics, so it just seemed like a natural fit. I definitely did not go to law school to snag a husband, but I do remember thinking on that first day that Scott was rather cute, with his Glen Campbell like haircut and his enormous brown eyes. We spent a lot of time together the first semester with our little group of wannabe lawyers. We both went out with others, but eventually drifted together and had our first date at a Halloween party. He got cold feet a few weeks into the dating process and announced,

"If you don't hear from me by Thursday of any given week, you can assume I've made other plans."

I responded by going to visit college friends in Iowa that very next weekend without informing him. When he called my home for that weekend's date, he was shocked I was not available.

Despite that inauspicious beginning, we soon found ourselves inseparable, and by July we were engaged. Scott and I both thought it was appropriate for him to ask for my father's blessing. He stayed up most of the night before the big day typing up a resume of his qualifications so he could answer any question Dad threw at him. He had a list of pledges defining how he would take care of me, always.

When the time came for them to have their talk, my father took him out to the side of our house where he tended a small vegetable garden. While Scott was professing his undying love and promising to provide for me financially, my father continued rotor tilling his patch of vegetables. My mother, sister and I were watching the scene from a bathroom window, which gave us our best view and a slight chance of hearing the words shouted over the deafening garden equipment. Scott need not have worried as champagne had been chilled for weeks anticipating this event. It was quite tasty with the tuna fish sandwiches that were hastily prepared as an accompaniment.

By this time, one year of law school had convinced me that this was not the career choice for me, and besides, I didn't really feel I needed a career anymore. I had a man after all. In my narrow 1970's viewpoint, I was content believing that most women still filled the traditional roles of teaching, nursing, and secretarial work; it was only the pioneers that entered into careers like journalism and broadcasting, medicine, law and the like. It was a very narrow view on my part, and if I have one regret in my life it is that I did not take law school more seriously or pursue a career in either print or broadcast journalism.

Wedding planning however soon took the place of property, torts and constitutional law. My mother and I commenced on an eleven-month whirlwind of dress shopping, flower selection, food sampling and band auditioning. Scott surprised and somewhat annoyed me by taking an active role in picking out china, silver and crystal. Today this is commonplace, but in the early '70's, it was most unusual for a groom to take an active interest in wedding selections. At some time in the process of floral selection, I decided I liked yellow roses. I did not know at that time that their meaning was jealousy; I just thought they were pretty. I am happy to see that the florist industry markets them now with a new meaning: joy, or new beginnings. How appropriate for a wedding flower; I was just before my time.

And so it happened that Scott decided to present me a yellow rose at the hotel on our wedding night. However, he ran into a little trouble. The day of the wedding, he purchased the rose, and put it in a vase on his front porch so he wouldn't forget it on the way to the church. His best man knocked it over. Another groomsman knocked it over again in his rush to return to the rental store to pick up some missing cufflinks. It miraculously survived its confinement in the limo during the reception. However, the hapless rose had more misadventures in store. My new bridegroom, now approaching his third year of law school, felt it necessary for us to sign Last Will and Testaments before we left for our honeymoon. So there we stood in the lobby of the

Marriott Hotel at O'Hare Airport with our best man and a bridesmaid, signing and witnessing wills where we gave everything we had (which was nothing) to each other. I do not think my new husband in his earnestness noticed the giggles emanating from the hotel check-in staff.

That chore accomplished, we proceeded upstairs to the honeymoon suite. In the excitement of signing my new last name for the first time, I left the rose in the lobby. Unfortunately, I remembered it just after we had both prepared for bed, and I insisted that Scott retrieve it. He looked at me like I had just dropped in from an alien planet, but wishing to indulge his new bride, got dressed and went downstairs. He was gone for a very long time. When we returned he was sans rose.

"Where is it?" I queried plaintively.

"It was gone. Don't worry about it. I'll get you another one when we get back from St. Thomas."

"No, I want that one. It's the one you got me on our wedding night. I want to save it. Please try to find it."

So downstairs he went again. This time he was gone even longer. When he returned, he said, not quite so sweetly this time,

"I still couldn't find it. But I have everybody in the hotel looking for it, and they have instructions to bring it right here as soon as they do. So, let's not worry about it okay?"

Well, okay fine. I could see he had other things on his mind. So we started enjoying our very pricey honeymoon suite. We sat at the dining room table, even though we weren't hungry, and had no food. We turned on the TV in the living room. Finally, we decided

29

it was time to go to bed. No sooner had we settled in, than there was a knock on the door.

"What in the world can that be?" he grumbled, now not disguising his irritation at all.

"It's my ROSE!" I happily giggled.

I made him get dressed...again...to answer the door. He had never imagined in his wildest dreams that the hotel staff would actually find the stupid rose, but find it they did. By the time he tipped the eager messenger, and presented me once again with the rose, it was well past three in the morning. Since we had a six am flight to the Caribbean and were exhausted from the day's activities, we voted to get some sleep. It was not the wedding night I'm sure he had anticipated.

Somewhere around the fourth decade of our marriage, I stopped getting those yellow roses. I don't know why, and I never asked. Maybe he just felt they were no longer a necessary way to celebrate. The last few years of our marriage were filled with stress over illness and employment upheaval and financial reversals, so a yellow rose may have paled in comparison. But for all the years he did bring them home, he brought me joy. And that, after all, is the meaning of a yellow rose.

7 CULINARY JOURNEY/THE DINNER PARTY

If you are going to do something wrong, enjoy it!

Yiddish Proverb

Our first dinner guests: our grandparents Jeanette and Elmer Anderson and Peter and Marcella Nickrandt

Displayed in a buffet that in its former life had been my husband's childhood dresser, our pristine crystal and silver wedding gifts gleamed. Eager to show them all off, I decided to host a dinner party in our honeymoon apartment. It was an ill-conceived idea from the start. First, I had not yet learned to cook. Oh, I could follow directions, and I made a mean peanut butter and jelly sandwich, but that was about the extent of my repertoire. When we were dating, I had once attempted to make veal fricassee for my beloved, but ended up throwing it out along with the pan to which it was forever glued. It was not my finest culinary moment.

However, armed with what my mother classified as a fail-proof recipe for beef roast, I was determined to pull off the social event of the season. Our first guests were to be our grandparents, as we each had a set living in the Chicago area. We did not invite our parents to this soiree, just the older generation. We wanted them to feel special, and besides, we didn't have room at our dining room table for more than six.

When the big day arrived, we got up early and went shopping for all the necessary ingredients. I am a painstaking list-maker; I have been known on several occasions to make a list of my lists. After shopping, we cleaned and scrubbed and polished every inch of our one bedroom apartment. I meticulously set the table with all our best wedding gifts: china, silver, crystal, all graciously reposing on a lace tablecloth. After all the fussing and preparation, I could put it off no longer. It was time to cook. Appetizers were cheese and crackers; no problem there. I could open a package of cheese with the best of them. The salad was easy. I chopped up some lettuce and tomatoes, tossed on some packaged croutons and had a bottle of ranch dressing handy and ready to go. The frozen vegetables reposed in a brand new pot, ready to steam their little hearts away. Baking potatoes glistened in aluminum foil coats, waiting their date with the oven. The rolls were a little trickier. I bought Pillsbury crescent rolls, and noticed that they baked at a different temperature than the beef was supposed to roast. I decided I would deal with that issue later. Dessert was a store bought cheesecake; I figured if there were any disasters, at least our sweet tooth would be satisfied.

Our guests arrived right on time. We proudly took them on a tour of our apartment, which took all of two minutes. We invited them to seat themselves in the living room. It must be noted at this juncture that we could not yet afford living room furniture. We had purloined two love seats from my parents that had been in their basement. However, they had also survived a flood, and their original thick cushions were tossed as a result. We replaced them with bright red velour fabric (over foam) cushions, only about three inches thick, which rested directly on the love seat springs. With everyone now seated, we offered beverages with our sumptuous cheese and cracker spread. My grandfather, now in his early seventies, requested a martini straight up. It was his drink of choice for an evening out. My grandmother had her usual, a whiskey sour. It always amazed me how fast she could down one of those, and promptly ask for another without missing a beat. Scott's grandfather had a beer and his grandmother a whiskey and water. As Scott entertained in the living room, I repaired to the kitchen to put the finishing touches on dinner. I decided (cleverly, I thought), that the rolls could bake after I removed the roast to "rest" and was preparing the gravy. However, disaster was about to strike. I took one look at the roast and panicked. It must have been a particularly lean cut of beef, for the pan was completely devoid of any drippings, and I had very detailed instructions on how to make gravy with pan drippings. I don't know if canned or jarred gravy even existed in those days, but I did not have any on hand.

"Scott," I called from the kitchen ever so sweetly. "Could you come here a minute, please?"

One look at my face told him that a disaster of incalculable measure was about to take place.

"What's wrong?" he practically shouted, or so it seemed to me.

"Shhhhh, they'll hear you. Look, there aren't any drippings to make the gravy. What should I do?"

Scott could solve anything. Especially if the solution involved his favorite thing in the world--wine.

"Just add a little wine. That will take the place of the drippings."

So I did. Only I added a lot of wine. Then I added flour to thicken it. However, the flour made it too thick, so I added more wine. Then more flour; and more wine. I saved only enough of two bottles to pour some in everyone's wineglasses. Candles were lit and everyone was asked to come to the dining room, a whole four feet away. No one, however, could get up. All four grandparents were wedged into the foam cushions, and my husband needed to physically lift them one by one to their feet.

That task accomplished, I held my breath and presented dinner. Within a moment or two, all conversation completely ceased. The only sound in the room was silverware scraping across dishes, and glasses clinking. At about this same time, I noticed that I was running out of crescent rolls. The Pillsbury packages held eight rolls each, and I had purchased two packages. That meant there were sixteen rolls for six people. And they were almost gone. My grandfather asked me if I had any more.

"That is the best gravy I've ever had," he said. "I just have to mop it up with the rolls."

Soon, everyone was doing the same thing. The conversation started up again, although no one was listening to any one else. Before long, they were all giggling. Now it was my husband's turn to ask for a conference in the kitchen.

"Did you cook that gravy at all?" he asked. "They didn't have THAT much to drink before dinner, and there was only enough wine left for one glass at the table. I think they're getting hammered on the gravy!"

"Well, I stirred it around some, but everyone was in a hurry to eat, so I guess maybe it still had some alcohol in it," I answered.

We both doubled over with laughter. We finished the rolls, and about half a loaf of white bread with the rest of dinner, until every last drop of gravy had been "mopped up." When it was time to offer dessert, they all declined.

"I'm just too full, honey," said my new grandmother-in-law, slightly slurring her words. "But this was the best dinner I have ever had. I want your gravy recipe, if you don't mind sharing it."

Everyone else concurred. My new husband excused himself to go laugh in the kitchen. We put on a pot of good strong coffee, and brought out our wedding album to kill some time while everybody sobered up before driving home. Our guests unanimously declined going back into the living room to sit on the foam cushions, electing instead to pass the album around the dining room table. While I was to host scores of dinner parties over the next several decades, rarely have any been as raucously successful as my first, thanks to my highly coveted gravy recipe.

8 PARENTAL JOURNEY/BABY, BABY

We never know the love of our parents for us until be become parents.
Henry Ward Beecher

 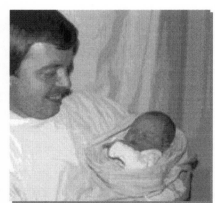

Ginger, 1974 and Kristy, 1978

It took me four trips to the hospital to get my two girls. I don't know why my husband and I felt it necessary to make a trial run each time, but we did. Practice makes perfect, I guess, but after each of the trials, I was determined to send the baby back where it came from. I had changed my mind.

Our oldest daughter was born a little over two years after our wedding. I worked in suburban Chicago near our home; Scott worked all the way downtown. Our hospital was also downtown. I was birthing this human, not him. Why did we not choose a hospital closer to the house? Because the doctor who was to deliver our daughter was also the doctor who delivered me, and I thought it was cool to have this multi-generational thing going on with her. That meant we were committed to a thirty-mile drive when the time came.

"Don't worry," she told us. "First babies always take their time."

I worked all the way up until the day before the blessed event. That afternoon, however, I was having some uncomfortable symptoms while sitting at my desk. It had never occurred to either of us that I might have this baby in the middle of the day when my husband and my hospital were both forty-five minutes away. We both just assumed the baby would come at night. Don't all babies?

I cancelled all of my boss's afternoon appointments, and told him I needed a ride. He took one look at me, bundled me into his Cadillac and sped down the tollway towards downtown Chicago and the hospital. My husband met us at the entrance and escorted me in, while my poor boss now had to face rush hour traffic driving back to the suburbs. After going through all the check-in procedures, I was placed in an examining room. By this time, the pains had subsided and I was feeling rather chipper. The doctor on call told me I had indigestion and to go back home. Thus ended trip number one.

When we got home, I went ahead with dinner preparations. Scott and I feasted on a sumptuous meal of beef stroganoff, Caesar salad, crusty bread and a bottle of delicious Cabernet. We topped it all off with generous slices of cheesecake.

Within the hour, I started having some discomfort again. Scott decided to play doctor and told me it must be the indigestion, and wondered why I had consumed such a large dinner. Giving him my best glare, I insisted this did not feel like indigestion.

One hour passed, and moans that came like clockwork every two minutes convinced him that I was not kidding. We grabbed my packed suitcase and headed once more down the highway system towards downtown Chicago and the hospital. Thirty minutes later, we both knew this was the real thing. The contractions were less than a minute apart, and were very regular. I thought all first babies took their time! Dinner had only been over for about two hours.

We had just purchased a new car, and Scott thought it would be better to park it in a safe place rather than leave it at the hospital entrance. There was a parking garage located across the street and about a half block from the hospital. So, instead of dropping me off, he drove up to the fifth floor of the structure and found a spot where the vehicle would be undisturbed. The elevator was not working, so we had to use the stairs. As we hit street level and hoofed it the rest of the way to the hospital, it occurred to me that I was nine months pregnant, in heavy labor, and had not only walked down five flights of stairs, but was carrying my own suitcase as well. My husband was carrying the car keys.

Asked to check in---again---we overheard several nurses muttering to themselves about the dumb parents-to-be who wait so long to come in. I refrained from telling them that I had been in their custody once already that day, and they were the dumb ones for letting me leave in the first place.

A nurse promptly plunked Scott in the Fathers' Waiting Room. Interestingly, there were no handles on the inside of the door. Once you were in there, you stayed in there until summoned. Within a short period of time our daughter was born healthy and without incident. The problem was that no one remembered to tell my husband he was a father. He stayed in that little room, listening to all the other fathers get their news, waiting for his turn. Finally, when a nurse came in for yet another new dad, he snuck out, and found me resting comfortably in recovery. He was displeased with the hospital services. I always felt it served him right for making me carry my own suitcase.

Little Ginger, however, was stunning; a Gerber baby if ever there was one. She made us make two trips to get her, but she arrived promptly and without too much hassle. I should have been more grateful, for it was not to be that way for daughter number two.

Three and a half years later, I was pregnant again. I finally had the good sense to change doctors and both the new physician and hospital were a mere fifteen minutes away from our house. As it turned out, that wouldn't matter, for this child decided to take her sweet time arriving. She was due around the first week of May, and we were now into week three, with June looming. On a Friday, I went for my checkup, and the doctor said that if the baby did not come over the weekend he would induce on the following Monday. That was fine with me. I went home, checked my bag for the umpteenth time and proceeded to try to enjoy my final weekend before becoming a mother of two.

That night as we were entertaining friends (it was spaghetti for dinner this time), I started feeling quite ill. Sick to my stomach ill. Violently ill. Figuring it must be indigestion (I am a quick learner), I ignored it as long as I could. Finally, we decided it would be prudent to go to the hospital. Our friends stayed with our daughter, and our odyssey began.

Before we got five minutes from the house, I got sick. Really sick, all over the car sick. When we got to the hospital, the admitting staff took one look at me and just put me into a room. No paperwork seemed to be necessary. I got sick again in that room waiting for the doctor. After as brief an examination as he could get away with, he pronounced that I had the flu. Instructed to go back home and come back on Monday to have the baby, I was a little miffed that the hospital wanted nothing to do with me. Then again, neither did my husband. I smelled bad.

By Saturday afternoon, the twenty-four hour bug had departed, and I was feeling much better. On Monday, I arrived at the hospital at the duly appointed hour and the doctor came to start the induction process. Then he left to see patients at his office across the street, instructing the staff to call him when I was ready. I tried to tell everyone that I had a history of short labor, but no one particularly listened. Big mistake.

This time Scott was allowed to be in the delivery room with me, as long as he ate first, then scrubbed and wore the proper sterilized garments. While some pretty nurse took him off to get a cheeseburger, another wheeled me into delivery. Upon examination, it was determined that this baby was ready to be born. Hadn't I just told them that? The doctor was paged and an intern showed up. The monitor started beeping wildly, indicating that the baby was in distress and the heart rate was dropping rapidly. I wondered what had happened to my husband; he certainly was taking a long time eating that cheeseburger. As it turned out, he was having his own troubles. He had been shown a linen closet and told to gown himself, put a sterile cap on his head, and booties on his feet. He got confused, however, put the bootie on his head and the cap on his foot, and wondered why he could not walk. After some poor orderly got him straightened out, he proceeded to the delivery room, only to hear the intern yell,

"Get some oxygen on her; that heart rate is plummeting!"

The next fifteen minutes were a blur, as the hospital staff tried to rescue a baby in big distress. My doctor showed up in just enough time to catch her like a football, while a very green-faced intern breathed a sigh of relief. Since she was a forceps delivery, she looked a little ragged coming out. Her head was shaped a little like a peanut, and she had scratches on her face. But to us she was beautiful, and our family was complete. Trip number four had been an adventure, to be sure. It was also probably the main reason there wasn't a trip number five or six.

9 FAITH JOURNEY/THE CHRISTMAS WISH

The golden moments in the stream of life rush past us and we see nothing but sand; the angels come to visit us, and we only know them when they're gone.

George Eliot

Ginger at age 6 with her Uncle Kerry

"**W**hat are we going to do?" I whispered to my husband. The anguish in his eyes conveyed that he had no answer to give me. Our seven-year-old daughter was perched on Santa's knee, and with heavy hearts, we both knew her wish was impossible. The recent drowning death of her sixteen-year-old uncle, with whom she shared a special bond, had devastated her, and she had not yet recovered. He had been a vibrant teenager, celebrating the end of school with his buddies, when he dove into a lake and never came up. The tragedy had shattered our little family, and particularly our daughter. This Christmas, Ginger didn't want dolls or toys. She wanted Santa to bring her uncle back. Knowing in her heart that was not possible, she whispered to Santa,

"But if you can't do that, I'd like to meet the Oak Ridge Boys."

The year was 1982. The previous summer, their smash hit, "Elvira" had burned up the charts - all of them - country, pop, even rock. Everyone, it seemed, was oom-pa-pa-mau-mauing along with the country superstars. They were the hottest act in the music business, and getting backstage to meet them was out of the question. We just didn't have the connections that were needed to get past the beefy security guards, the hordes of fans camped in the hotel hallways or the heavy steel backstage doors that shut with a decisive thud after the band and their entourage had passed through. That night after Ginger and her three-year-old sister, Kristy, were safely tucked in bed, we brainstormed.

"Perhaps if we write a letter to their office, maybe someone would make the arrangements," suggested Scott, not sounding at all hopeful.

"Maybe if we order some merchandise, like tour jackets or tee shirts, that would be an alternative," I offered.

But we knew in our hearts that Ginger needed something very special to try to fill the hole that her uncle's sudden death had left. My husband and I finally agreed that treating them to a show might be an acceptable gift. At least we could get them in the same room as the performers. Maybe we'd even try to slip a note backstage and see if the girls could be acknowledged. So the next morning, I called for tickets to the Oaks' New Year's Eve performance, at a venue about ninety minutes from our home.

"I'm sorry, ma'am" was the rather brusque voice at the other end of the line, "but that show has been sold out for months now."

When the line went dead, so did any hope of fulfilling a child's dream. The days ticked by towards Christmas, and we knew our little girl was going to be disappointed, her faith shaken. She had lost so much that year; it broke our hearts to know that her Christmas wish would also go unanswered.

Just as things looked their bleakest, the first miracle occurred. While cleaning house one day, I turned the vacuum cleaner off just in time to hear an announcement on the radio.

"When the next Oak Ridge Boys song starts playing, the first caller to reach us will win four tickets to their show on New Year's Eve!"

I sat by the radio, the phone clutched in my hand, for about forty-five minutes before I heard it. The song, appropriately enough, was entitled, "Thank God for Kids." I dialed as fast as I could, amazingly enough got through, and the tickets were mine. Even little children must know when wishes to Santa are difficult to fulfill, for the tickets left under the tree thrilled our daughter.

"Wow, Mom, look! Santa couldn't exactly have us *meet* the Oak Ridge Boys, but we get to go to a concert to see them. How cool!"

It seemed to be enough.

Both girls also received beautiful handmade matching dresses from their grandmother that Christmas. They were the perfect gift for this special night out. At the concert, Ginger and Kristy looked like little princesses, adorable visions with long blonde curls, enveloped from head to tow in gowns of deep blue velvet and ivory lace. Vendors were selling scarlet roses in the lobby of the theater, and their Daddy proudly presented each of his little girls with one. We took our VIP seats in the second row, and settled in to enjoy the performance. After a song or two, the girls noticed that others in the audience were bringing flowers to the stage.

"Mom," whispered Ginger, "Can we go up too?" I nodded.

"Sure honey. But hold your sister's hand."

Shaking with nervous anticipation, they timidly approached the stage with their flowers. The oldest thrust hers at tenor Joe Bonsall; the youngest held hers out for baritone William Lee Golden. They were rewarded with kisses on the cheek from the singers, and laughter and applause from the audience. They literally floated back down the aisle to our seats, eyes sparkling and grins spreading from ear to ear.

I whispered, "Thank you, God." If it had ended there, it would have been enough.

But we were to have no idea what was set in motion that night. An unexpected ice storm precluded us from driving from the Indiana venue to our suburban Chicago home. So we stayed overnight at the hotel adjoining the theater. How they still had a room available on New Year's Eve, I will never know. The next morning, a woman with long, blond hair approached us.

"Hi," she said. "My name is Tysh and my husband is the sound engineer for the Oak Ridge Boys. We were all watching last night from backstage, and thought your girls were just adorable. The Boys would like them to have some autographed pictures. Would that be all right?"

I thanked her and assured her that it would indeed be all right. For a brief moment, I thought about explaining Ginger's wish, but I lost my nerve. We chatted for a few more seconds, then she almost blurted,

"You know, I think I can get you some backstage passes to meet the singers if you would be able to stay for tonight's show."

The impossible dream was becoming reality.

We did go backstage that weekend, and everyone treated us like royalty. The Oaks, their wives and everyone on their staff fussed over the girls. Had that been the end of it, it would have been enough. But for nearly forty years, we have been proud to call the singers, their wives, their kids, their band and their crew, our friends. Any time their tour came near our area, we were invited. Many members of the group have been guests in our homes, both in Illinois and Arizona, over the years. Their music may have been the catalyst that introduced us, but we became friends because of the values we shared. We shared an abiding faith in God, we had the same goals for our children, we enjoyed helping others, we were all proud of our country and the people who served it. Like all relationships, there have been both good times and bad. We have laughed together and we have cried together. The friendships have been tested, but have always endured. One night, with the Oaks on the verge of a painful breakup, Ginger, now on the brink of adolescence, looked tearfully into lead singer Duane Allen's eyes.

"Duane, I'm just so afraid that I will never see you again," she said.

Duane put his arm around her and responded,

"I promise you that I believe all things happen for a reason, that God will work things out for the best. I want you to believe that, too."

It was a powerful lesson, and she has never forgotten it.

For more than three decades, we've shared our hopes and dreams and late night pizza all over the country. The little girl who sat on Santa's knee that December long ago conducted her first interviews for a class project in third grade with Joe Bonsall and Mark Hunt, the sound engineer who started it all. She is now in upper management with a major newspaper. She has won numerous journalism awards along the way and interviewing high profile individuals has never fazed her. Her younger sister, at the ripe old age of four, perched herself on Duane's lap one morning at breakfast, spilled his coffee (to her mother's horror), kept on smiling, and was rewarded with a laugh and a hug. Since then, she has never been afraid of anything. As a very young child, she provided a spark on several years of home videos that we made as a family for the group. Now armed with a degree in broadcast journalism and political science, she has held jobs as a television producer, a staffer for a United States Congressman and the President of the United States, and is now a communications director for a global healthcare company. Joe Bonsall wrote college recommendation letters for both of them.

Looking back, we had no idea what that impossible wish to Santa would bring, but maybe our daughter, through her beloved uncle, had the right connections all along. No one will ever convince me that God did not intervene that Christmas, and grant a wish to a little girl that changed our family's lives forever. Blessings cannot be choreographed; they often come when least expected and need only be accepted with gratitude.

Ginger and Kristy backstage with the Oaks, circa 1996

10 CULINARY JOURNEY/BIRTHDAY CAKE AND JELL-0

Laugh at yourself first, before anyone else can.

Elsa Maxwell

One of my infamous birthday cakes

O ur youngest daughter's first job after college was as a producer for a TV station. When she occasionally worked weekends, my husband and I would often bring dinner for her and her co-workers, as it was difficult for them to search out food on a Sunday evening while they were trying to generate a newscast. We catered a full dinner, enough to serve about thirty people, and usually planned a casserole or Italian dish, bread, salad and dessert. The meal, however, never included cake or Jell-O, even though both could serve a crowd and were easy to prepare and transport. There was a very good reason for this. I have never been able to make either.

As our kids were growing up, two things struck terror in my heart every calendar year. The first was the annual passage of their birth dates. The second was the foreboding lament of "Mommy, I don't feel good."

The latter was a cry that came approximately three times annually, from each child. Factoring in the two birthdays, my remedial math skills told me that I was set up for humiliating culinary failure at least eight times a year. For that reason, I always dreaded birthday parties and the flu.

Tradition had it that each child chose the type of cake she would like for her birthday. This could vary between yellow with chocolate icing, white with chocolate icing, chocolate with chocolate icing, even marble cake with chocolate icing. You get the idea. It was my job to go to the store, buy a boxed cake mix, and pre-made (uh, chocolate) frosting in round plastic tubs, a bunch of candles, a couple of eggs, oil, and some decorative icing in a contrasting color. It sounds simple, doesn't it? Well, it did to me too until I actually had to do it. As instructed, I began the ritual by greasing and flouring the round 9-inch layer pans. This entailed getting my hands all goopy with Crisco, rubbing the inside of the pan and covering every rounded bend. Next, the directions instructed me to "dust" the pan with flour. The flour inevitably "poofed," then dribbled all over the kitchen, landing not only in the pan, but on the counter, the floor, the refrigerator, the walls and on me.

Next, it was time to unite the rest of the ingredients. To the cake mix, I would add the eggs and the oil, and some water. With great flourish, I would activate the mixer. Then I would watch the mix billow throughout the kitchen, onto the counters, the floor, the refrigerator, the walls and me. Of course, if the cake mix was white, I inevitably was wearing black; if the cake was chocolate, I was wearing white. After finally getting enough liquid blended with enough dry stuff to keep most of it in the bowl, I would release the conglomeration into the greased and floured pans, scooping the inevitable spillage with a batter-coated finger, and kneeling on the floor to make sure the amount of mixture in the pans was precisely even. Next, after wiping batter off my knees, and with the preheated oven waiting, I sent the little round would-be cakes to baking heaven. Martha Stewart would have been proud.

The next step was the excruciating wait of 25-35 minutes while the treasures inside the oven transformed themselves. The birthday child would usually sit cross-legged on the kitchen floor, anxiously maintaining surveillance over her special treat. The dog would sniff, his tail wagging. Time seemed to stand still. When the oven timer finally pierced the silent anticipation, and the delicious sugary aroma filled the house, happiness reined. The birthday child and I, now being scrutinized by the slightly pouting other sibling (whose birthday it was NOT) would cautiously open the oven door, remove those precious little delicacies and ever so tenderly place them on a rack to cool. Just like the package said.

Now came the amusing part; getting the suckers out of there. The pans were gently turned, and tapped on their bottoms, knife eased around their sides. One pan usually performed just fine, and it always seemed to be the first one. Then it was time for that annoying second layer. Even though it had been greased, floured, mixed, beaten, and baked exactly like its twin sister, this second little devil always seemed to come out of the pan in chunks, or lopsided. Every single cake looked like either the ruins of the Acropolis or the Leaning Tower of Pisa. The birthday child's glee transformed to tears.

"Don't worry," I soothed. "I can fix it."

I'd reach for my trusty remedy, whispered to me one day in secret by my mother-in-law, and perfected over many years of such disasters. It was a box of instant pudding, in the same flavor as the frosting.   (Utilizing incredible foresight, I always purchased pudding mix at the same time I purchased cake ingredients.) The gelatinous consistency acted just like glue, and even though one side of the cake contained enough pudding to choke a horse, the layers bonded together and the cake always appeared reasonably level.

The crisis came when it was time to cut the cake. We all knew that one of the lucky little neighborhood kids was going to get a huge mouthful of chocolate pudding. Now chocolate pudding is a culinary delight, enjoyed by millions every day of the year. However, when you are expecting chocolate frosting, pudding is a poor substitute. It's sort of like when your mouth anticipates fish and gets sushi. It may be in the same family, but it is definitely not the same taste! We could always tell when it happened. Expecting frosting, the greedy little child would dig right into the gooey mess. Immediately, his or her face would contort into something akin to those in the Bitter Beer commercial, and the little darling would either spit it out, or yell, "This isn't a birthday cake; it's yucky!" Every year, twice a year, the story repeated itself. Every year, twice a year, I watched my children shrink in humiliation, secure in the knowledge that their mother's incredible streak of cake disasters was intact. Thinking back on it, we should have had a little pool going, and taken bets on which kids would get the pudding slice. That way someone could have at least had a monetary benefit.

As dreadful as the cake adventures were, the Jell-O saga was ghastly. At least the cake represented a cheerful occasion. There were usually other distractions, like balloons and presents and games to entice the little ones from the cake disasters. However, when a child is ailing, and has just come from hanging her head over the porcelain bowl, sense of humor seems to disappear in direct proportion to impatience rising. At this particular time, a child only requires two things. She wants her Mommy and she wants to start feeling better. The Mommy part I could do. I could cuddle them, and I could fetch cold washcloths and aspirin. I could read books, or play endless games of Chutes and Ladders.

Helping them feel better by getting a little something in their stomachs was not as easy. My kids wanted Jell-O when they had the flu. They would start with sips of a soft drink, but that lost its appeal very quickly. Jell-O was like graduation to real food again. It meant they were getting better. Only I could never, EVER get it to work. How challenging could this possibly be? You acquired a bowl. You opened the package. You emptied the contents of the package into the bowl. You added water, hot and cold. You stirred the mixture. You deposited the bowl in the fridge. Voila. You created Jell-O. Only I never did. I created mush. I do not know what I did wrong. In an attempt to correct my shortcomings, I made Jell-O side by side with my mother, my husband, and both of my children. I did exactly what they are doing. Their Jell-O jelled; mine did not. Theirs wiggled and shimmered in the bowl. Mine shimmered, then fell limp, oozing towards the outer reaches of the receptacle. When the kids were sick, I would present them with their Jell-O, whatever flavor they requested. Only I served it with a straw. As they got a little older (just past toddler stage), they had the wisdom to ask their father to make it. Worse, they would rise from their sickbed and make it themselves. Do you know how humiliating it was to watch them drag themselves, pale and spent, feverish, in their footy pajamas to the kitchen and start pulling out the bowl and the package of Jell-O? Yet, I would observe, fascinated, as they went about their business, and an hour later, dig into a big bowl of jelled Jell-O. It was amazing.

Both of my daughters have their own homes now. When they get sick, they might allow me to provide an occasional bowl of chicken soup, but neither will ever ask me to come over and fix them Jell-O. As for the birthday cake problem, I've solved that too. I have found that grocery stores and bakeries have them for sale. How cool!

11 PARENTAL JOURNEY/SWIM MEETS, DEBATES AND CHEERLEADING (OR HOW I SPENT MY FORTIES)

Kids spell love T-I-M-E.

John Crudele

My fortieth birthday

A S my fortieth birthday approached like a European bullet train, I began to get apprehensive. For years, I had heard that life began at forty, but I was not convinced. All I could think about was wrinkles and cellulite and needing reading glasses. I must have whined sufficiently for long enough that my husband felt it prudent to come up with something that might help me forget my impending decline into old age. He hit the jackpot. At a family dinner celebrating the big day, he presented me with a beautiful white mink jacket. That in itself knocked the socks off me. But nestled inside one of the velvet-lined pockets was a diamond tennis bracelet. If this was the forties, sign me up, because I felt like a princess.

It was the last time I would feel like a princess for the better part of a decade, for I was about to become very busy. Being forty meant that I was a mom with a teenager and a fifth grader; a mom who just happened to own a mink coat and a diamond bracelet, not normal attire for the life that was about to become mine.

That same fall, our older daughter had entered the wonderful world of high school. As a freshman eager to conquer the world, she plunged head first into as many activities as she could possibly handle. The high school swim team was looking for participants, and when they announced they would not make cuts, Ginger decided that this might be the outlet for her. Even though she had never swum competitively before, she was an excellent swimmer and decided to give it a try.

Our high school did not have a pool, so practices were held at a community pool not far away, five days a week, rain or shine. Practices lasted for a minimum of two hours, and the times varied each year because several other schools were also using the same pool for their practices. One year, our school might practice from three to five pm; the next year it might be seven to nine pm. Thirteen-year-old high school freshmen do not yet have the privilege of driving, so it was incumbent upon us as her parents to get Ginger to and from practice every day. There were days she got rides from others, but until her junior year, those were few and far between. Driving back and forth to practice was the easy part, however. The actual swim meets were an entirely different story. Held once a week, they could be anywhere: the community pool, or another pool in another district clear on the other side of the Phoenix metropolitan area, or even downtown Yuma clear on the other side of our state, three hours away. Most of the facilities also did not have bleachers or seating of any kind for spectators. Therefore, it was not an uncommon sight to see a clump of middle-aged adults, having raced from work still dressed in suits and ties and dresses and heels, standing around on the pool deck dodging splashes of water coming from the pool. It was not a prudent place to wear a mink coat. Meets lasted about two hours, and the kids not only raced against each other, but also tried to improve their personal best each time they swam.

If the conditions for watching were not the best, the competitions were usually fast-paced and interesting. Sometimes it got just a little too interesting. One time during her freshman year, Ginger decided it would be fun and challenging to have a small asthma attack while in the water. She was swimming laps when all of a sudden her lungs started closing up on her. Gasping for breath, she was one of several people in the pool at that time, and no one was particularly paying any attention to her. She started flailing around until finally another member of the team noticed her discomfort, dove in and dragged her to the side of the pool. The coach was oblivious, as were the rest of her teammates. What could have been a serious incident turned into a small case of puppy love when my daughter looked languidly into the eyes of her rescuer – a tanned, dreamy-eyed senior. She never complained about going to practice after that day.

But try as she might, and practice diligently as she did, our daughter seemed to have an unusual issue when she was in the pool. She got lost. The three years she was on the swim team, I don't think I ever saw her swim in a straight line. She would start out just fine, arms pumping in windmill fashion, feet kicking ever so delicately just under the water and head turning from side to side seemingly effortlessly; then she would start to stray. First, she would head towards the lane markers on the left; then she would overcompensate and head towards the ones on the right. She would zigzag her way down the entire length of the Olympic size pool, make her turn and do it all over again. We understood then why she never posted winning times; she was swimming twice the distance of anybody else! She was always a trooper, though. She may not have been the best swimmer on the team, but she made many friends, learned how to be a team player, and showed a lot of heart.

However, by far the worst punishment inflicted on us as parents during her high school years was Speech and Debate. By the time Ginger had reached her senior year of high school, she had been on the swim team for three years, was active in various club activities, and was editor of the newspaper and the yearbook. She realized her talents were leaning towards writing, so she decided to cap off her high school career by joining the Speech and Debate team. To this day, I am not sure how I survived her decision. Speech and Debate was the club name for the National Forensic Society, a nationwide organization that promoted competition in a variety of speech forms. Some of the categories included policy debate, public forum debate, Lincoln-Douglas debate, duo interpretation, dramatic interpretation and original oratory. There were strict rules for each category. Our daughter's topic was: "Not Guilty by Reason of Insanity; Why the Plea Should be Abolished." The rules of the competition stated that there were to be three rounds. Further defined, that meant that each participant gave their speech or debate or interpretation three times before a different set of judges each time. At the district or state level where dozens of schools send representatives in the various categories, that meant that hundreds of students were earnestly delivering their presentations in triplicate. All the points from all the rounds from all the judges were added up to determine the winners. Needless to say, this made for a very long day, and night. It was not unusual for us devoted parents to arrive at the host school at ten a.m. in the morning and not leave until around midnight. There were two positive aspects for me, however. While I never was able to wear my mink coat to any of my daughters' school activities, I did wear the diamond bracelet to more than a few speech tournaments. I discovered I had more than enough time to count the diamonds and polish each and every one of them several times. By the time the results were announced, my jewelry was gleaming. More importantly, our daughter won her category at the state level and was able to go on to the National tournament her senior year. Her father and I couldn't have been more proud. Unfortunately, we were unable to make the trip to Fargo, North Dakota. Yes, North Dakota. Previous years, the national finals had been in California, Washington, D.C., Boston and even Hawaii. The year she qualified it was North Dakota. Nevertheless, it was a crowning achievement and a great experience for her.

As her high school years ended, I was not about to sit idle. It was time to gear up for cheerleading. No sooner had Ginger graduated from high school, than Kristy was ready to start her freshman year. Eight consecutive years of high school is an endurance contest for parents and should not be entered into by the faint of heart. Our younger daughter started her cheer career in eighth grade and continued it all through high school, with a brief intermission with the swim team when she was a freshman. She also joined enumerable clubs and became the second of our daughters to be yearbook editor.

With cheerleading, however, we were about to get an education. We noticed very quickly that there were strict rules associated with this sport, and do not be misled; cheerleading is most definitely a sport. Rule number one (which would also manifest itself several years later in sorority life) was that if more than two girls gathered for any given function, a new tee shirt needed to be purchased to commemorate the occasion. Rule number two was that wardrobe discussions were mandatory before any cheerleader stepped out of her home into the public eye. Our phone was constantly ringing with members of the squad calling to discuss whether they would wear the cute white bow, the cute green bow, or the cute gold bow with the green vest or the white skirt or the gold sweater and the green skirt. Once wardrobe was settled, the most rewarding part of cheerleading for the parents was sitting in the stands during Friday night football contests, watching with pride as their progeny, ponytails whipping from side to side, cheered the team to victory. Sometimes we even watched the game.

However, for every pleasure, there is a price. For cheerleading parents, that price was the competitions held twice annually. First there was a regional competition held in the fall; second was the national competition, which in our case was held in Anaheim, California every spring. It didn't matter what they were called or where they were held, however. They were mind numbing. First came the preparation. Rehearsals and practices were usually six days a week, for a minimum of three hours each session. Additional conditioning took place at a gymnastics facility. This would not have been so bad had it been limited to the off-site locations. Our Kristy, however, felt the need to practice at home as well. There was rarely a waking minute when we did not see her go through the house either stamping her feet, clapping her hands or kicking high into the air, or trying all three simultaneously. This activity would usually also be accompanied by either loud pulsating music or the dog barking in time, or both.

The day of the competition, the ozone layer was breached as thousands of teenage girls emptied hundreds of cans of hair spray, and primped, curled, ironed, tucked, teased, and otherwise made themselves magazine cover perfect. Finally, it came time for the actual competition to begin. The squad from each local high school competed against a minimum of twenty others for bragging privileges and a trophy. At the national level, this number was multiplied at least five-fold. Each team or squad did a three-minute routine, set to pulsating recorded music. There was about a two-minute break and the next team would compete. I do not believe I ever heard more than two different songs in all the competitions I attended, and all were played at Mach level. Hours, and I do mean many hours later, all squads finally had their moment in the limelight. Those that felt they had done well held hands in a tight circle and giggled amongst themselves. Those that had dropped a girl during a lift or had otherwise messed up were in another corner sobbing as though they had lost a favorite family member. Then we sat. For what seemed like an eternity, we waited for the judges to come back with their decisions. When the winners were announced, their high-pitched squeals drowned out the sniffles from the losers. Everyone took this competition very seriously, at least for about an hour or so. After that, pizza usually solved all the problems of the world. Meanwhile, the parents were drained not only of emotion, but also of hearing.

We were one of the lucky few families who also got to experience individualized cheer competition. Each year the state would crown a state champion cheerleader, the best of the best. It was sort of like a Miss America pageant for cheerleaders. Judging was based not only on the physical prowess of the cheerleader, but on academics and personal interviews as well. Watching a child compete with a team is nerve-racking; watching her compete all by herself in the center a huge coliseum is terrifying. Kristy, however, was the essence of calm. She knew her 4.0 average was the highest of all the competitors, and her less than timid personality had helped her in the interview, so all she had to do was go out there and perform. Perfected by months of practice at school and in our living room, her routine was flawless, and she walked off with the State Championship Trophy. Mom and Dad could only beam.

After four years of swimming, one year of speech, three years of cheerleading, clubs too numerous to count, a newspaper editor, two yearbook editors, two National Honor Society inductions, a National Speech finalist and a State Champion cheerleader, my forties were drawing to a close. If I felt that they had approached with the speed of a bullet train, they went by with the speed of lightening, way too fast to dwell on a few wrinkles or the need for bifocals. If my husband's thoughtful, beautiful gifts had made me feel like a princess, my daughters' gifts of teenage exuberance and taking me along for the ride made me feel like a queen. I wouldn't have traded all the practices, all the meets, all the competitions, and all the waits for results for even a fraction of a king's ransom. I had all the riches I could possibly handle.

12 LESSON JOURNEY/THE ACCIDENT, THE INCIDENT, THE DRIVE, THE DREAM

Honor isn't about making the right choices. It's about dealing with the consequences.

Midori Koto

Tailgate party before the big game, December, 1994

A rizona isn't Texas. The high school football competition here is not a religion. No one has ever written a treatise about our Friday night lights, like the one that chronicled the Midland-Odessa team some years ago, describing their obsession in all its glory, warts and all.

But that is not to say that it is not important here. Arizona is a state made up of people from somewhere else; Illinois, Nebraska, New York, Minnesota, Iowa. It is filled with millions of inhabitants who gave up the snow and cold to bask in the Arizona sunshine. These folks also gave up their roots and their neighborhoods and their old dreams to fulfill new ones in the desert southwest. The price they paid was often a nomadic feeling. To counteract that, new traditions had to be created, new alliances had to be shaped, new friendships had to be forged. High school football was one way to do that. Cheering on the local team gave people the sense of community that most of them were seeking. True, folks had to sit in the stands in September in shorts and tee shirts at 8 pm while the temperature was still well past 90 degrees. (By October, it might have cooled to a chilly 80 degrees). Nevertheless, it was still football, it was still their kids, and it still brought them together.

Therefore, it was with anticipation in their hearts and aspirations of glory in their souls, a special team from the north side of Phoenix, Arizona, began the 1995 season. I had a ringside seat because my daughter was a varsity cheerleader. It proved to be a memorable autumn. The August newspapers said it all. The Horizon High School Huskies were the team to beat. Under the leadership of Coach Doug Shaffer, this group of almost all veteran seniors had the capability to win it all, to become state champions. The press clippings were quite impressive; they spoke of the quickness of running back John Clayton and the sure hands and strong throwing arm of Jeff Voigt. Jeff had the talent to scramble as well, and the media touted him as one of the best quarterbacks in the state. The offensive and defensive lines were enormous, averaging over 250 pounds, bigger than even the professional Arizona Cardinals team. So the seed was planted and the dream began to take form.

School was about to start; the last few days of freedom dwindling down for youngsters who now dreaded the drudgery of classrooms, rules and confinement in the searing temperatures of an Arizona fall. So on one particular day, quarterback Voigt and three of his fellow teammates were enjoying the last moments of a carefree summer. A summer where all they really had to worry about was making those tortuous practices in the muggy 115-degree heat. As Jeff drove home, the unthinkable happened. Maybe the music on the radio was a little too loud; maybe he was joking with his buddies and not paying attention. Maybe it wasn't his fault at all. It didn't matter. He had an accident. The three passengers in his car were uninjured, but for minor scrapes and bruises. But Jeff Voigt, the quarterback and cornerstone of the Horizon football team, suffered a broken collarbone, literally days before the start of the promising new season.

Word spread around school like a death in the family. This was supposed to be "their" year. The press clippings said so. The first game was a non-conference event against powerhouse Mountain View High School from Mesa. Even with Jeff out of the lineup, the Huskies were cocky. They had that number one ranking, after all. Reality smacked them in the face in the guise of a sloppily played, 21-2 loss. They won their second game, however, and began to believe the press clippings again. Since Jeff was still sidelined, they took this as a good omen. Games three and four produced one more win and one more loss. Jeff returned for the fourth game, although he still wasn't at one hundred per cent. Playing .500 ball after four games was not how this season was supposed to play out. Now the local papers started to call them overrated. Panic didn't exactly set in, but a sense of apathy did.

And that lead to the Incident. It happened just after a regular daily practice session. The team was in the locker room charged with the duty of studying films of the opponent for the upcoming week. When the coaches momentarily left the room, one of the players substituted another video for the film tape: a pornographic video. When a coach unexpectedly came back in and discovered the switch, the punishment was swift and sure. All but three members of the varsity squad had remained in the room to watch, and Coach Shafer made a decision that not many coaches intent on winning a championship would do. He could not condone the behavior or the lack of discipline, so his decision was to suspend the entire team for the upcoming game. Except for the three players who left the room, the junior varsity squad would play on Friday night.

The local press had a field day. Reporters and camera crews and TV vans camped out at the school to get sound bites from everyone from Principal John Stollar to the custodial staff. It was the lead story on all the evening newscasts for days. The Arizona Republic published a cartoon showing Horizon football players gripping a video entitled, "Holly Does Horizon." Even Paul Harvey's radio program and Jay Leno's Tonight Show had features on the "Incident at Horizon High School." Doug Shafer had punished his team, and made a point; however, it was commonly believed that he had probably sacrificed the season as a result. The kids became celebrities of sorts, but with a young, inexperienced roster taking the field, they were about to lose another game, 29-3.

The suspended players witnessed the thumping from front row seats in the stands, and it was a dejected bunch of young men who boarded the school bus that night for the long ride back to Horizon. It is said that adversity builds character, and this misfortune was no exception. The team seemed to draw together after their humiliation; they played now for a common purpose. For whatever reason, they reached deep inside themselves and decided it was time to live up to those early press clippings. They had learned a costly, yet invaluable lesson from their coach in what was expected of them and taking responsibility for their actions. Now they had something to prove. The rest of the season they went undefeated, and without exception beat their remaining opponents by lopsided scores. In the balance of their regular season games, they never scored less than forty-two points.

They won their division and entered the playoffs. In the first round they won another lopsided victory; in the quarterfinals they exacted revenge on first game nemesis Mountain View; and in the semi-finals, they beat a powerhouse team from South Phoenix. Of all the teams that had started the season with dreams of grandeur, the Horizon Huskies now found themselves with only one obstacle in their path to a State Championship; the Knights from St. Mary's Catholic High School. The dream was but one hurdle away from reality.

The night of December 9, 1995 at Sun Devil Stadium on the Arizona State University Campus was frigid and cloudless.

Temperatures hovered at forty degrees, rather chilly for an Arizona evening, even in December. The stars enveloped the heavens. It was the 5A High School State Championship Game. Mothers adorned in the jerseys of their player sons beamed with pride. Dads barbecued hot dogs and hamburgers for the tailgate party, and alleged the smoke was responsible for the moistness in their eyes. The mothers knew better. As game time approached the crowd filed into the stadium where most had witnessed many football games over the years. This stadium was the familiar home not only of the college team, but also at the time, the state's professional one as well.

Tonight, however, the field belonged to the high school kids. The Huskies stormed the stadium resplendent in their forest green jerseys. The cheerleaders' gold and green pompoms shimmered in the stadium lights. Their pony-tailed hair swayed to the sounds of the high school band as drums and trumpets blared the school fight song. The field seemed bigger; the lights brighter somehow as over fifteen thousand freezing fans took their places in the stands. At least half of these souls shivered not just from the cold, but also from the anticipation of watching the Horizon Huskies play in their first ever state championship game. Students with bare torsos, braving the cold, stood in a line, the paint on their bodies spelling out H-O-R-I-Z-O-N H-U-S-K-I-E-S. They shared space in the stands with neighbors and friends bundled in ski jackets rarely removed from closets. The harsh clapping of the kids' hands contrasted with the muffled sound of the gloved palms of the adults. But those differences didn't matter. This was a community that had truly come together as one.

In the opening quarter Horizon drew first blood with a two-yard handoff pass from quarterback Jeff Voigt to running back John

Clayton. The scoring drive went sixty-one yards and ate up 5:49 on the clock. A second quarter field goal by Scott Finkbeiner and a touchdown pass by St. Mary's made the score 10-7 as the teams went into the locker room for half-time. Horizon finished the half with one hundred ninety-eight yards to St. Mary's eighty-five and controlled the ball for eighteen and a half minutes to St. Mary's five and a half. Yet, in the statistic that counted, only three points separated the teams. St. Mary's dominated possession in the third quarter, but there was no additional scoring. However, in the fourth quarter, St. Mary's scored another touchdown, going ninety-six yards and using almost eight minutes of the clock. They now lead the contest, 14-10.

Receiving the kickoff, Horizon smothered the ball on its own twenty-yard line. There were eight and a half minutes to go in the game. On first down, they lost a yard. Second down brought a gain of six. On third with five yards to go, running back Brooks Tyree barreled through the heap and just made the first down. There were seven and half minutes left. Tyree plowed into St. Mary's territory. Clayton had an eight-yard run to the St. Mary thirty-seven yard line. Now just over five minutes remained. Tyree scampered to the twenty-nine, gaining another first down. Tyree carried again, to the twenty. The clock showed 4:06. Tyree took a handoff to the nineteen. "Keep it on the ground and churn out the yardage," bellowed the coaches. Voigt carried for a short gain. It was second down, with the ball on the seventeen-yard line. Tyree pushed to the thirteen. At third and four, Tyree got two more. The clock showed 2:25 remaining, with fourth down, two yards to go.

Everyone in the stadium was on their feet. The noise was thunderous. Clayton jumped over the pile, made the first down and a couple extra. It was first and goal! Jason Paoletti broke to the left to the three-yard line. Now there was only 1:12 on the clock. Pandemonium was breaking loose. Most of these kids had grown up together, played Pop Warner together, and now found themselves in the final seconds of an incredible football game. Clayton was hit from the side and fumbled, but by some miracle, the ball popped right into the hands of his teammate, Jeff Johannson. There was no gain, but Horizon retained the ball. There was also no gain on second down, with fifty-five seconds remaining. Now it was third down and only thirty-one seconds left. Unbelievably, a blunder was made and Horizon was called offsides for a five yard penalty.

Low moans could be heard from the stands. They sounded like the distant thunder of an approaching Arizona monsoon. Then it was silent; on both sides of the field. It was fourth down, seven yards to go. Horizon had to go for it. The whole season was right here, right now. The incredible clamor from the stands started up again. Jeff rolled to his right and was tackled at the ankles. He started going down. It appeared to be happening in slow motion. The collective gasp that came from the Horizon side of the field was deafening. Jeff was falling, falling. Suddenly, he shoveled underhand to Brooks Tyree, who stood poised just one footstep away from the goal line. Brooks looked stunned, but somehow managed to swallow up the ball and put his foot over the line. TOUCHDOWN HORIZON!!! The Score was 16-14. Pandemonium reigned on one side of the field; heartbreak on the other. The game wasn't quite over yet, however. The Horizon kids were penalized for celebrating and missed the extra point. Since St. Mary's had the premier kicker in the state, they still had a glimmer of hope for a field goal. But with only seventeen seconds left to get far enough down the field to make the attempt, their last ditch Hail Mary pass resulted in an interception. The contest was over. Horizon had won its first ever state football championship. The Dream was reality.

Ironically enough, that final game turned out to be a microcosm of the entire season. First there had been the tantalizing promise of victory, with such high hopes. Then there was adversity and all seemed lost. In one final miraculous finish, there was triumph.

Many years have passed since that extraordinary night, since that unforgettable season. Horizon has been back to the "dance" but has not repeated as champions. The members of that team have gone on to jobs and families and dreams of their own. What did they take from that night? Hopefully they remembered all the things those few fall months in their lives embodied. Hopefully they remembered the lessons they learned, the coach that stood up to them, the parents that supported them, and the character they found in themselves. Hopefully they remembered that even though they didn't think so at the time, their coach gave them a remarkable gift, just as they gave their school and community a glorious season. Hopefully they remembered the magic of that night and the long winding road that led them there. And hopefully they remembered the cheers. They earned them.

State Champion Horizon Huskies

13 VOLUNTEER JOURNEY/IF YOU BUILD IT, THEY WILL COME

You must give some time to your fellow men. Even if it's a little thing, do something for others - something for which you get no pay but the privilege of doing it.

Albert Schweitzer

Seniors enjoying their all-night graduation party

One of the most rewarding things in life is to make something out of nothing. It matters little if it is writing a song or a story, building a house, starting a business, or planting a garden. The point is that individuals, through hard work, imagination, and determination can make life a little better for themselves or others by creating something new.

Such was the case with Farewell Fiesta. An article in the paper one spring morning in 1991 caught my eye. It described an all night party in another state for graduating seniors that was meant to replace private parties where alcohol might be served. Alarmed by the recent number of deaths and injuries at our own high school over the past several years, I thought this was a great idea. Not all these tragedies had happened at graduation, but five members of the class of 1991 were lost over the course of their four years to alcohol related incidents. My own daughter was due to graduate the following May, and I wondered if this kind of party wasn't something we could pull off at her school. Almost immediately, however, my rational mind kicked in, and I thought of all the reasons why it wouldn't work: our school was so big, over two thousand students, with more than five hundred in the senior class alone. It would be impossible to organize such an undertaking. In addition, it would require a lot of money, and I had no idea how to raise that much. We would need the administration's cooperation, a task easier said than done. Most importantly, I feared the kids would never buy into it. They had been looking forward to graduation night and all the rowdiness it entailed for four years now. They would never elect to attend an on-campus party with no drinking. Would they?

Try as I did to put the whole crazy idea out of my mind, it kept popping back in. It turned out that in a couple of weeks, a school not too far away was going to try such an event for the first time. I called their chairman and was informed I was welcome to attend, but I needed to work a shift, not just observe. So on graduation night, I gathered my husband, the somewhat reluctant principal of our high school, a handful of my daughters' friends, and off we went. Scott and I were assigned coke duty; that is, we poured soft drinks for two hours. After our shift was over, we were allowed to wander through the rest of the party to see how things were going. I took some notes, but mostly just marveled at the smiles on the graduates' faces. Here they were, back on the high school grounds for one last time with all their classmates. They weren't drinking, and they were having fun.

The seed had been planted. Since Scott and I were already members of our high school Booster Club, we presented the idea of starting our own party on our campus. We were met with cautious enthusiasm. The other parents had the same concerns that we did regarding administrative cooperation, raising money and student attendance. We decided the first step was to talk to our principal. John Stollar was not only a fine administrator; he was a personal friend. After listening to our proposal (and having had the experience of seeing those kids at the neighboring school), he gave us his blessing. It was lukewarm, however. He said, "If you want to try this here, I'll help you any way I can. But I doubt it will work at this school."

With that ringing endorsement, we began. To be fair, John would do anything that would be to the benefit of "his" kids. He just had the same concerns we all did. I asked one of my good friends to be my co-chairman. I was a little frightened to take on a job of this magnitude by myself, and Chris was just the right complement to me. I saw the overall picture; she was great at details and ideas. We decided to have the party on campus for a number of reasons. First, graduation itself was held on campus, so it was easy for the seniors to attend. Secondly, our school was perfectly designed for such a party, with an open courtyard surrounded by classrooms on one side and the cafeteria on the other. Third, and most important, it was free.

Scott cajoled his law firm into making a $250 donation, which became our seed money. We recruited other like-minded parents to be chairmen of the various committees we felt we would need to pull off this venture. We needed folks in charge of food, activities, decorations, volunteers, prizes, security, first aid, publicity and of course, fundraising. We broke the major committees into sub-committees to involve not only more parents, but also to lessen the burden on everybody.

To counteract the concern about the seniors not wanting to attend we came up with a plan: the party would be absolutely free of charge to them, they could bring guests if they wanted, and they would be free to leave the party at any time they wished. There were two caveats: they had to sign a pledge card that they were drug and alcohol free, and they could not win a prize if they were not present. Then we decided to appeal to their greed. We solicited donations for pizza, hamburgers, sodas, pretzels, ice cream, and all the other foods that teenagers love. We also canvassed the community for prizes. Our goal was to have a door prize worth between $10 and $20 for every one of our five hundred seniors, as well as other larger prizes throughout the evening.

That first year we gave away trips to Disneyland and Hawaii, $1000 cash, a computer system, stereo equipment, televisions, a set of tires, and scores of gift certificates. Some of the prizes were distributed by raffles, others by auctions. The auction prizes were purchased with "Husky Bucks," which was play money the graduates earned by playing various games. Our auctioneer was Principal John Stollar, who I think had as much fun in his role as the graduates did watching him. We planned carnival games, casino games, and various other contests that could help them add to their bankrolls. Volunteer parents staffed each of these activities.

When it became obvious that not all the food and prizes and activities that we required were going to be donated, we looked for ways to raise money. We approached corporations in our community and asked them for contributions. We received money from our school's Student Council, and the Booster Club donated funds from the football concession stand. However, we still needed more, and we were adamantly opposed to charging the seniors to attend. We decided to approach the senior parents for a donation. We thought that asking each senior parent for a small ($20) amount of money might appeal to their sense of security in providing a good party for their kids. Despite both a letter writing and phone campaign, the money was not rolling in, so we played the "greed" card again. This time we sent out postcards informing the parents that any student whose parents made a contribution by a certain date would get double the play money to start the evening, thus giving that student a head start on winning the prizes. We hit pay dirt. Before long, we had met, then exceeded our budget, and were able to beef up the prizes even more.

Only one question remained, and it was the big one: would the seniors show up? Graduation night arrived on the wings of a freak monsoon storm. In Arizona that usually means dust storms and high winds, often accompanied by torrential rain. These storms are commonplace in August, but not in May. During all our planning sessions over the year, we had never considered a contingency for bad weather. We lived in Arizona, after all. I could barely focus on the graduation ceremony for my daughter because I was so worried about the party into which we had put so much of our hearts and souls.

I found John Stollar just prior to the processional, just as he was donning his robe, and asked desperately,

"What are we going to do if it rains?"

He replied with a wicked grin.

"Hey, my job is to give diplomas. You're on your own, kiddo!"

Seeing my stricken look, he put his hands on my shoulders and said,

"It'll be fine. You built it, and they will come. It won't rain, but if it does, we'll deal with it."

We got lucky. We got dust and wind, but no rain that night. The party was on, but it still remained to be seen how many kids would actually show. My job that night as the chairman was to rove the party and oversee all the other committee members and their stations. My own daughter, being one of the graduates, was mortified to think she would spend her graduation night with her mother hovering over her every move. She admonished me prior to leaving for the school that evening.

"Now, Mom, if you see me there tonight, just walk the other way. You don't need to keep coming up to me and asking if I'm having fun, okay?"

Okay. At ten-thirty p.m., we were ready for action. The entrance was staffed, the hamburgers were grilling, the games were in place, the prizes were on display, and the DJ was playing music that pulsated throughout the campus. I stood near the entrance with my co-chair, Chris, and waited. A few seniors came down the walkway and started to sign in, but only a few. But soon there were a few more. From our vantage point we could see the school parking lot, and the street beyond. My friend looked at me with tears in her eyes, and said,

"Oh my goodness, LOOK."

As far as we could see were the headlights of cars winding their way towards the school. It looked like the scene from "Field of Dreams." Indeed, we had built it and they HAD come. I spent the rest of the evening in a whirlwind, visiting games and food stations and overseeing prize distributions. On at least three occasions, my newly graduated daughter sought me out. This was the same daughter that had earlier asked me to stay away from her.

"Mom, look what I won!" "Mom, I love that Husky race game!" "Mom, can you believe the pizza is FREE?"

If I needed any validation of my efforts, I had just received it. The party that night was a rousing success, and continued in its original format for over a dozen years. Over the course of that time, over $250,000 was raised, with almost all of it going back to the kids in the form of food, games and prizes. Over four thousand members of our community volunteered their time to work either that night or during the year, averaging more than three hundred each year. Attendance of the senior class routinely averaged in the ninety-plus percentile. The statistic that was most satisfying, however, was that not one of our students were hurt or injured on graduation night during all those years. The state of Arizona now boasts scores of all night graduation parties, held at high schools and other venues all over the state. Horizon's Farewell Fiesta was the template for many of them. We started with nothing and created something very special. There is no better compensation.

14 DEPRESSION JOURNEY/INTO THE DEPTHS

Depression is like a constipated rhino sitting on your chest.

Rob Anderson

With Richard Carpenter in Japan, 1996

When my oldest daughter decided to go off to college a thousand miles away in Texas, I steeled myself for the ever-dreaded Empty Nest Syndrome. I bought books about "letting go" and studied them religiously. I filled our September calendar with social engagements and volunteer activities so I would be too busy to notice she was gone. When we made the long drive out to Ft. Worth and moved her into her dorm room, it was my husband who insisted we circle around the block six times to try to catch a final glimpse of her in the window of her room. I was happy for her new experiences, and while I knew I would miss her, I realized that this new phase in her life was exciting and right. Besides, I was busy being the mother of another teenager just starting high school, and our house was a never-ending stream of giggling girls, telephone calls, and activity. I would gladly tell any of my friends who had children about to leave for college that it was not an ending, but rather a liberation of sorts, a new lease on life. I patted myself on the back, and threw away the "letting go" manuals.

I should have held on to them. Four very short years later, we were attending two graduations within the space of one week. One daughter was graduating from college and the other from high school. I was also trying to absorb the blow that the little baby I had sent off to Texas was not coming home: she had accepted a job at the Ft. Worth Star-Telegram as a reporter. Although I was extremely proud of her, I couldn't help thinking that this had not been part of my game plan. Going off for a four year adventure to Texas had been one thing; taking up permanent residence there was completely another.

Soon it was time for the youngest one to leave as well. Unlike her sister, she decided to go to a state university, one that happened to be located a mere twenty minutes from our front door. She was planning on living on campus, and I never gave her departure another thought, since she would be so close. That is, until I came home that night from helping her set up her dorm room. The flash flood that erupted on Scottsdale Road as we drove from Tempe to our home was nothing compared to the tempest going on inside of me. I shook it off as best I could, but just like a storm of Mother Nature, it was not to be denied.

It should be noted that this was the autumn of my forty-eighth year, and unbeknownst to me, my body was also planning for some changes of its own. Within a few short weeks, forces I could not seem to control buffeted me about, and I started tumbling into a dark abyss. When my youngest daughter broke up with her high school sweetheart and boyfriend of two years, I thought she had ruined her life. When my older daughter starting dating a Marine, I thought he was the devil. (I was right about that). When my husband tried to defend either of the girls, I lashed out at him. I cried all the time, and a lot of the time I didn't even know what I was crying about. My sister told me she was worried about me; my mother tried to talk some sense into me. I could not hear their words or see the anguish on their faces. Someone suggested counseling. I refused. What did they think I was, nuts? Everyone was picking on me, all the time, and I wanted them all to just plain leave me alone.

I went to work at the travel agency every day, and robotically went through my chores. I came home and prepared dinner and watched TV and did normal things. But I certainly wasn't happy. Too many nights I cried myself to sleep, or in the alternative, lay awake praying that God would stop my misery. I didn't particularly care how He chose to do it, either.

Three things saved me. First, my husband and the other members of my family didn't abandon me. They might not have liked the person I had become, but they hung in there, although I'm sure there were times they regretted the misfortune of having to be related to me.

Secondly, email had just burst forth on the scene as a viable way for ordinary people to communicate with each other. I had a few friends across the country that I kept in close touch with. They had no idea what I was going through (since I didn't know what it was either, I never shared it with anybody), but their emails always cheered me. The frequency and immediacy of the communications alone made me feel not quite so lonely.

Third, I went to Japan. Working in a travel agency gave me an opportunity to meet a very interesting older gentleman, who at one time had been a big time entertainment manager. He was semi-retired and living in Scottsdale when he came into the office with his Bichon Frise and asked for a ticket to L.A. I made a fuss over his dog, and he took a liking to me, becoming a regular client. Before too long, he asked me to book a first class trip to Japan for a client of his who was going on tour over there. There were to be forty members of his entourage. We worked on this trip for over a year, and I eventually discovered that his client was Richard Carpenter, an icon of the seventies music world. One week before the departure, one of the members of the orchestra was unable to travel, so my client asked me if I would like the ticket. Somehow I knew this was the life preserver I needed, and I jumped at the opportunity. I spent six days in Japan while Richard was performing in Tokyo, and it was my magic pill. I spent time with Richard and his family, I watched his shows from backstage, and I dealt with whatever emergency travel issues came up. During the down time I toured the city by myself. I figured out the Tokyo train system, and experimented with sushi. I was almost fifty years old, but I was gaining a confidence in myself that I had never had before. I could be more than a wife and a mother, even though those were my two most important jobs, and I wouldn't trade them for anything.

I know now that the combination of children leaving home and pre-menopause is not pretty. Little did I know that this episode was a precursor for a much deeper, debilitating depression that was to occur almost twenty years later. Should I have sought counseling? Perhaps. But for me, at least this time, counseling came in the form of the love of my family, a steady stream of email and springtime in Tokyo.

My backstage pass

15 HISTORICAL JOURNEY/A DAY IN NORMANDY

Never, never, never believe any war will be smooth and easy, or that anyone who embarks on the strange voyage can measure the tides and hurricanes he will encounter. The statesman who yields to war fever must realize that once the signal is given, he is no longer the master of policy but the slave of unforeseeable and uncontrollable events.

Sir Winston Churchill

American Cemetery overlooking Omaha Beach in Normandy, France

The SS Norway was nestled in its berth. The gleaming cruise liner had crossed the English Channel during the night, gliding through the seawater almost effortlessly. As the new day began, it disgorged its passengers through a cavernous opening on the starboard side. They looked so tiny as they filed out and strolled along the huge cobalt blue and brilliant white hull. Fifteen hundred people, on vacation, off to see France. Many would head into Paris, some three hours away, and spend the day strolling the Champs-Elysees or taking in the view from the Eiffel Tower. Others would take an organized tour from the ship to the Normandy beaches, site of the D-Day invasion that was the turning point of World War II.

Although the weather was dreary, with the ominous skies threatening rain, everyone was in a holiday mood. This was the last port of a ten-day cruise, where luxury and pampering had been a daily routine. The passengers were relaxed, well fed and anticipating this last full day of vacation. My husband and I were two of those cruise passengers. Having been a history major in college, and born only a few years after World War II, I couldn't help but think of the crossing of this channel decades ago, and how my generation was the one most directly impacted by what had happened here.

That other crossing had not been so idyllic. Rough seas, cramped boats, seasickness and fear had all taken their toll on the young kids making the trip. They had to wade through waist high water to make it to shore. Many never made it at all. Those that did faced hell on earth.

Traveling is one of my greatest joys, and cruising is a passion. We had looked at this trip as just another vacation, albeit a nice one. We were about to find out, however, that it would come to mean much more.

After disembarking, we grabbed a taxi and headed into the town of LeHavre and Hertz Rental Car. After securing the vehicle, which was no bigger than a large tin box, we headed west on the superhighway. Our mission that day was to visit the Normandy beaches and battlefields, one in particular. We didn't want an organized shore excursion, where we would be bussed with fifty other passengers and driven in air-conditioned comfort to the sights. We didn't want to share this with anybody. We were there to try in some way to follow the path of one particular soldier, to see what he had seen, to try to understand, to try to pay tribute.

Our first stop was the city of Caen, about a ninety-minute drive. Caen was the gateway to the Normandy beaches, and is now the home of the Memorial for Peace Museum. The flags of every country involved in the Second World War encircled the grassy knoll by the front door. Their brilliant colors stood in sharp contrast to the somber tones inside the museum. Its contemporary, cavernous halls chronicled the failure of peace after World War I, and the subsequent rise of totalitarianism. Immense rooms showcased the spread of the war, the D-Day invasion and the Battle of Normandy. Television monitors flickered with grainy black and white images of newsreel footage from a past generation. Miniature scale models were everywhere with little toy soldiers and diminutive tanks representing the actual human forces and machinery.

So much manpower and equipment, so many young men. But the soldiers that waded up the beaches and scaled the cliffs and claimed the countryside inch by inch that incredible day were made of genuine flesh and blood, not plastic.

From Caen, it was a short thirty-five mile drive to the beaches. Driving along the coastline, both of us were struck by the quiet beauty of the landscape. The small town of Honfleur, with its colorful terraced homes on the hillside, overlooked the water. At one time it had been a favorite hideaway for the artist Monet; now it was a popular tourist village. Deauville was next, another charming seaside town. The sun began a battle with the clouds, breaking through with rays of light on the beach. The sand was a creamy white, the ocean the hue of blue topaz shimmering where it met the land. Further out, the water turned to a dark sapphire blue.

We approached the famous beaches; Juno, Sword, Gold, Omaha, Utah; code names for the strips of land that became the beachheads for an invasion.

How could it be so pretty? What must it have looked like that day? Equipment and bodies and blood staining the white sand. Time had sanitized the beaches and eradicated the destruction. Hopefully time would never erase the memory of what they did here.

We stopped for lunch at a small seaside restaurant just at the edge of Omaha Beach in the town of Grandcamp-Maissy. There were four tables on a back porch overlooking the sea. We feasted on fresh mussels, with a gentle breeze from the ocean cooling the early afternoon temperatures. The breeze also brought with it a mild aroma of fish and salty air. Three other couples also enjoyed lunch on the terrace; one from Australia, one from Germany and one from England. The proprietors spoke only French, but we managed.

The GI's didn't enjoy a fresh ocean breeze. Instead, they suffered through acrid smoke and fire and blood and sweat and other odors we probably could not even imagine. They probably didn't even get to eat lunch that day. If they did, it sure didn't taste like this. If the invasion had never taken place, what would this spot, this very spot, be like today? Would we be ordering our food from a German menu? Would any of us even be here?

Mussels consumed, it was time to continue our journey. Next stop was the American Cemetery, situated high on a bluff overlooking Omaha Beach. It reminded me of Arlington National Cemetery with an ocean. It was simply breathtaking and simply heartbreaking. A semi-circular colonnaded Memorial faced a reflecting pool and the graves of almost ten thousand American soldiers. The main pathways were laid out in the form of a Latin cross, each gravesite marked by either a white marble cross or a white Jewish star. The perfect, neat rows continued for as far as the eye could see across impeccably manicured emerald green lawns. The seashore below rivaled any Caribbean beach resort for its beauty. Every grave had a view of the beautiful sea below. It was fitting that their final resting place was so serene and peaceful.

Some of the men buried here must have been the buddies of the soldier we were here for. I wondered if somehow they might know we had come to honor them too. They sacrificed so much so that we could stand there that day. Did they know how grateful we were? They never were able to live their lives or realize their dreams or raise their children or grow old with their wives. We are in debt to them all, and it was impossible to keep the tears from falling as we paid our respects.

But the day was wearing on, and we had one important place to visit before returning to the pleasant sanctuary of our cruise ship. The objective of our pilgrimage was to visit the modest inland town of St. Lo. Just outside of this town there had been vicious fighting, for St. Lo was a key to the ultimate goal of the liberation of Paris. We again squeezed into the tiny vehicle and spread out the map we had purchased at the museum in Caen. Ironically enough, the map was in German; all of the English ones had been sold. This very fact was going to make it a little difficult to find our way, since neither of us spoke nor read German. It was also not lost on either of us that had it not been for the fighting that took place here, we might be fluent in that language. Coupled with the fact we often misplaced ourselves while driving (a term preferred by my husband to "lost"), it became obvious after a short period of time, that we would need help finding our destination.

The roads were narrow and winding. It was impossible to go very fast. In order for two cars to pass, one had to pull over to the side of the road. Before too long we came upon a Frenchman, purposefully pedaling his bicycle up a rather steep hill. He looked as though he had been dropped into the twentieth century from a time capsule, or perhaps was an extra on a period movie set. He was dressed all in black, a lightweight turtleneck over black knickers. Black socks, and elf-like slippers completed the ensemble. A black beret was perched on his head, and the basket of his bike held a long baguette of bread. We pulled over to the side and attempted to ask directions.

"S'il vous plait, monsieur...la directiones a Saint Lo?" In long forgotten high school French, my pronunciation was "Saynt Low."

The French gentleman gave a quizzical look. He looked at the German map, and to the name of the town where I was pointing.

JOURNEYS OF A BOOMER

He must really think we are crazy. Here were two obviously lost Americans in the middle of nowhere, way off the beaten tourist track, asking for directions in very broken French with a German tour map. We will probably be dinner conversation at his home tonight. Crazy Americans.

"Ahhhh, Saan Lu" he responded.

Okay, if you say so. Now that the destination was clear, our tour guide launched into no less than a five-minute explanation of how to get there, gesturing wildly as he spoke. We understood not a word.

"Merci," we said.

As we continued, my husband asked, "Did you get any of that?"

"I think he said 'la gauche' somewhere in there, I replied. "It means turn left."

So we did. Less than a kilometer later was a sign that directed us to St. Lo. The drive there was breathtaking. The sun-splashed French countryside was in its full glory this early September day; for by now the sun had won the battle with the clouds and the promise of a glorious afternoon awaited. As I pulled out my sunglasses, I couldn't help but think how the weather of this day was, ironically enough, a metaphor for that one so long ago. It had started so drearily, and with such foreboding. By days' end, the sunshine of renewed hope had taken hold; the promise of freedom had broken through the clouds.

In the late summer sun, everything was green; so many shades of green. The light yellow-green land was a tapestry of small fields and farmlands woven together by miles of hedgerows. The verdant trees, lush with leaves, gently blowing against a bright blue sky, contrasted this quilt of nature. The hedgerows were striking. Neatly trimmed and maintained, they were a dark forest green, like someone had taken a thick magic marker and outlined everything. They formed the fences of all Norman fields, and lined every roadside and lane. Each patch of land looked to be no bigger than an American football field, and hedgerows surrounded every single one. We saw miles and miles of these small fields with their high, bushy barriers on the way to St. Lo.

How terrifying it must have been for our soldiers, for the man whose path we were following. The German enemy hid in these bushes, waiting to ambush our troops. How these very hedgerows must have been ripped apart by mortar fire, the tree trunks shredded with shrapnel, and how our soldier must have burrowed himself in ditches and foxholes dug desperately into the landscape. How brave he must have been.

We approached the town. At first glance, it was disappointing. I guess we were expecting a charming village, set in another century. But this town looked modern; its buildings were formed of yellow and gray brick. Its unimaginative, squared off architecture, the steel and glass, looked like something out of the 1950's. Then it dawned on me; this town WAS out of the 1950's. Most of it had been destroyed in the war, and it was completely rebuilt in the decade following.

In stark contrast to the new, there was one ancient building that stood tall and proud in the middle of town. It was the Church. Called Eglise Notre Dame, it was centuries old. The entire center section of the church had apparently been blown away, for its reconstructed replacement was a flat, unadorned bridge between the sculpted original sections on either side. The rest of the building still consisted of the old stone and mortar that was laid down hundreds of years ago with intricately carved arches and statuary. However, unmistakable to the eye were the pockmarks from mortar shells, the statue of Jesus with his head blown off, and deep gouges in two of the sides of the building. The good people of St. Lo had decided to leave the scars of war in this monument to God, and that is appropriate. No one that visits could ever forget what happened here as they gazed upon this House. This visual said more than a thousand treatises on peace could ever have hoped to.

As we walked around town, we began to see its beauty. It was not a physical beauty, although there had been an attempt to plant flowers and gardens, and the stores and homes were certainly well maintained. The beauty was in the people, who when they realized we were Americans, greeted us like long-lost friends. It was in the simple acts that were performed in the town everyday; children playing in the park, couples holding hands while they strolled the streets; shopkeepers going about their business. They had their lives back and their futures intact because of what happened here a generation ago.

They lived in freedom because of men like the one we came here to honor. He was just one man, one American GI, but for us, he was the symbol of a great crusade. We never met this GI; he was a name and a few photographs. But we knew his son, and we had heard his story. We know he was gravely wounded somewhere in these fields; we knew those wounds were with him all the rest of his life. The ravages of war affected not only him, but his family as well. A wife, a son and a daughter were all shaped by the demons that followed him home. He left a piece of himself here; a piece of his soul. But he also helped to free a world from tyranny. We live our lives the way we do because of the sacrifices he and his friends made here. What a legacy he had given us all. His was one of thousands of stories. An entire generation of America's young men and women laid their lives on the line so that future generations might live in freedom. The Greatest Generation gave the rest of us the greatest gift.

It was time to head back to the ship. As we drove through northern France to the coast and back to the port of LeHavre, it was quiet in the tiny little car. We only got "misplaced" once. We each had our own thoughts, but it was a day neither of us would ever forget. We knew we were better for having come here this day. I hope somehow that the one we came here for and all the others knew that their sacrifices here were important. I hope they knew that the magnitude of what they did here can never be measured, nor ever adequately acknowledged. They may not be famous; few will know their names. But they are true American heroes. Although we never met them, we will always hold them in our hearts. They represent what is good and true and right about this country we call home. They were ordinary people who did an extraordinary job and helped save the world in the process. Thank You, GI Joe. God Bless you, always.

16 LEGACY JOURNEY/DAD

The words that a father speaks to his children in the privacy of home are not heard by the world, but, as in whispering galleries, they are clearly heard at the end, and by posterity.

Ricther

My Dad with his family, 1990

L to R: Marian Anderson, Robert Anderson, Kristy, Scott and Holly Richardson, Steve and Bill Kaiser, Ginger Richardson, Katie and Dawn Kaiser

Dad and Mom just a few months before his death, 1999

B oom!!! Boom!!! Boom!!!
I shuddered as the reports rang out, even though I knew they were coming. Seated under a ramada, I was shielded from the warm April morning sun. The military unit from Luke Air Force Base was at attention to my left, and I watched them raise their guns for the salute. I knew the noise was coming. Even so, the loud cracks in the still air startled me. My father's funeral. How incredibly surreal. Dad had been sick for a long time, so I knew it was a blessing that his suffering, and my mother's as his caretaker, was finally, mercifully over. But how would I be able to live my life without him watching me, approving, suggesting, loving? How could he be gone? My mind drifted. Wasn't it just a few spring times ago that I was a little girl?

Memories are funny things. Sometimes they are so vivid you can recall every detail, every color, every smell, and every sound. Other times they are just a vague recollection, like a cloud that wisps through the sky and then just as quickly, vanishes. Most times, they are somewhere in between. You remember the rudiments, but the fine points can be a little foggy or can change with the years. Sometimes photographs or someone else's recollections of the same event bring memories into focus. But whatever form they take, the album of those memories tells the story of a family, like a finely woven ancient tapestry.

I remember there was always music. Now that's sort of a funny thing to say, because Dad couldn't carry a tune in a bucket. I inherited that trait. My mother had a beautiful voice; unfortunately she did not pass it on to me. I don't even like to listen to me sing. But when I was small and didn't know any better, I used to love to belt out a good song. My sister and I would warble away in the backseat of our Buick when we were little, on the way to our grandparents' house. We would sing the whole score from "The Music Man", and we each had our own parts. (I was especially proud of my rendition of "76 Trombones" and the Irish accent I perfected when Marian's mother sang about "liberries").

Now Dad might not have sung very well, but he did play music. His first instrument was the accordion, which he played as a kid and young adult. Soon he added the piano and organ, and even led a band during the forties. There always seemed to be music playing in our house. If it wasn't Dad playing, it was the radio or the old 78 records of Louis Armstrong or Patti Page, or even Theresa Brewer. When I was growing up, my folks belonged to a bridge group called the Unholy Twelve, which met every month. When it was Mom and Dad's turn to host the party, it always seemed to me, tucked away in bed listening to party cacophony, that the bridge playing soon ended and the songfest (no doubt fueled by a few Martinis, Rob Roys and Manhattans) began. Dad would play the organ in our living room. He'd usually start out with "Goofus." I don't think I ever heard any words to that tune; I don't know if there are any. But he played it just about every time he sat down to play; "Goofus" was a staple for fifty years! There would usually also be a rousing rendition of "If You Knew Susie." Sometimes I would clamber out of bed, and stand in the living room in my pajamas, one hand on my hip and the other clutching a teddy bear, asking them to quiet down so I could get some sleep; but secretly, I loved those parties. They were one of the sounds of my childhood. Those parties were a microcosm of 1950-60's middle America; young couples sharing time, relaxing together, having fun, enjoying their lives.

As a very small child, I remember standing on my father's feet as a three year old as he shuffled to my favorite song, "The Blue Waltz." There is an old 16mm silent movie of me in a red velvet dress with white lace trim, grinning from ear to ear, while he guided me around the Christmas tree. Some nineteen years later, I tried to avoid his feet as we danced together to "Daddy's Little Girl" at my wedding reception.

Every once in awhile, however, Dad would give in to the urge to burst into song. Just a few weeks before our wedding, Mom and Dad had hosted a party for my bridesmaids and their families. With the impending wedding of his firstborn approaching as quickly as the bills stacking up on his desk, Dad enjoyed himself and his beverages that night. After the last guest had left, we found him prostrate on his favorite lounge chair on the deck of our house overlooking the golf course and lake, singing "Everything is Beautiful" at the top of his lungs. After a couple of foiled bids to get him to bed, Mom just left him there to spend the night. To the best of my recollection, he pretty much stuck to playing music rather than singing after that.

The last time I heard him play was Easter Sunday, 1999. We usually went out to brunch as a family on that holiday, but that year Dad was weak from cancer and diabetes, and both Mom and he agreed that it would be best to have brunch at home. So the family congregated, putting on its best game face. As I rang the doorbell, I thought I heard the organ playing. But no, that couldn't be. Dad was just too ill for that. He barely was able to get dressed and walk from the bedroom to his favorite blue chair by the television, where he stayed almost all day until it was time to go to bed at night. There he was, however, perched at the organ, a grin as wide as could be. He was playing "Easter Parade." His encore, of course, was the inevitable "Goofus." Mom said he practiced for weeks. He died two weeks later. It was his last gift of music to us all.

My father was a man of simple principles. He believed in honesty, hard work, making your own way in life, and accepting responsibility for your actions. He loved his country and was very patriotic. Those beliefs manifested themselves in the way he lived his life. Very conservative, he was a champion of the Republican Party, for it seemed to embody best all that he believed in. My first recollection of a presidential campaign was 1956, Eisenhower vs. Stevenson. I remember my folks being elated that Eisenhower was beating Stevenson in a landslide, even though the latter was from our home state of Illinois. My eight-year-old intellect figured that all was still right with the world, and I snuggled deeper into bed, secure in the knowledge that my life would go on, happily uninterrupted.

The 1964 campaign was also particularly memorable. I was sixteen, a junior in high school. Our school hosted a debate featuring students who supported the two candidates, Goldwater and Johnson. I espoused the virtues of Barry Goldwater. My opponent's name was Marshall Johnson. Although he was no relation to the President, he was, however, a very good debater and formidable opponent. We went at it in front of the whole school and a reporter from the local paper. My mom and dad were both there, too, cheering me on. I remember thinking that if I did well enough, I might just be able to swing this election Goldwater's way. That of course, was not how it worked out. On election night, I was inconsolable. Just as my eight-year-old mind thought Eisenhower's re-election made things all right; my much more mature sixteen year old intellect figured Goldwater's loss meant the end of civilization as we knew it. I went to bed sobbing. It was my Dad, who, after letting me cry it out for awhile, came in and explained very gently that even though our candidate had lost, it didn't mean that our principles had lost. We would still hold them true to our hearts. The sun would come up in the morning and the world would go on. And of course it did.

Dad didn't just pay lip service to his convictions. He, and Mom too, believed that service for the public good was more important than their own self-interests. They tried to make their world a little better. Dad served as President of the PTA (Mom even got him to dress up as a clown for a fund-raiser); President of the School Board, President of the local Bar Association, Kiwanis President, Mayor of his town. All of those positions were voluntary, without pay. He always was a community leader, trying to improve his little corner of the world through his talents, his time and his contributions. He was definitely one of those "thousand points of light" that George H.W. Bush often spoke about.

The central focus in his life, however, was always his family. We were a small bunch, with not a lot of relatives on either side. We shared Thanksgivings, Christmases, Easters, birthdays and graduations together. Attendance at these events was not optional. Even when my sister and I were teenagers and had other interests or preferences, it never occurred to us to try to get out of a family gathering.

When it came to our immediate family, Dad took an active role. I don't recall him ever changing my little sister's diaper or vacuuming, but he was always there, physically and emotionally. He never missed a play or a parade or a recital. We had dinner together, every night. When I got married and had kids, our family did that too. I sometimes think that many of the problems this country has today could be solved if families just sat down to dinner with each other.

Most families have their traditions. Some of ours were a little stranger than others, of that I am sure. The appearance of Santa Claus every year was one of them. Now I know that millions of American children believe in Santa Claus and anticipate his arrival every year. But his arrival at our house was unique, to say the least. This tradition was actually started by my grandfather, but my experience began with my Dad. At an appointed moment every Christmas Eve, the doorbell rang. Two excited little girls ran into the bathroom and closed the door so as not to see the magic unfolding. Yes, the bathroom. I never really understood exactly why that room was chosen, but I suppose it might have been because it was the room with the nearest access to the living room where all the activity was about to take place. Santa then stomped around the room, asking my sister and me if we had been good little girls all year.

"Yes, of course!" we answered back, and the conversation was on. Mom and Dad joined in, exclaiming about the bounty that Santa was leaving under the tree each year. Santa and Dad talked about reindeer and cookies and having a safe trip. My sister and I sang "Jingle Bells", usually followed by "Silent Night," because that was my mother's favorite. If we felt like being obnoxious, we launched into "The Twelve Days of Christmas." I think I was about seven or eight before I finally discovered that Santa was Dad, and Dad was Santa, and he was actually carrying on a entire conversation with himself. Meanwhile, Mom raced around putting presents under the tree. The most bizarre (or

wonderful) part of this whole tradition is that it has continued through the generations as first my children and now my grandchildren anticipate Santa's arrival and a songfest in the bathroom every Christmas Eve. Each father has taken his turn "talking" to Santa over the years.

Dad enjoyed games, too. His favorites were golf, bridge, baseball and Frog. Frog was a pool game he played with his grandchildren, my girls Ginger and Kristy, and their cousins, Steve and Katie. All four got into it with him. Even though our girls were a little older and thought they were way too sophisticated for Frog, I knew they enjoyed this game with Grandpa. It had simple rules. Dad would swim underwater and come up behind one of the kids and pop up, yelling "ribbit, ribbit." The chosen child would squeal with delight. Frog would go under water again and one kid (or four) would try to get his attention next. This went on for as long as Grandpa had breath and stamina. A silly little game, but all four of them will always remember it.

Dad was funny. He wasn't a stand up comic by any means; in fact, he was usually a terrible joke-teller. One of his most famous attempts at a joke gone wrong occurred when I brought a new friend home from college my freshman year. Determined to make Linda feel at home; Dad cooked ribs (I think he burned them), and when we sat down for dinner, decided to tell his joke about Charlie. Now we all had heard this joke a million times, and it was rather funny. Dad launched into it, embellishing each stage with words and descriptions. He went on and on. Linda was taken in, listening with rapt attention. And still dad kept building to the climax. The joke was about this guy named Charlie who bragged to his friends that he knew everybody in the world. The punch line found Charlie on the papal balcony at the Vatican and was supposed to be "Who is that guy with his arms around Charlie?" My dad, however, after all the preambles, with everyone waiting for what was sure to be a hysterical climax, took a deep breath, and said, "So who is that guy with his arm around the Pope?" Linda politely laughed, and dug into a crisped rib. My mother, sister and I were hysterical. When we pointed out to Dad what he had done, he too broke into one of his belly laughs, where his whole body shook with laughter and tears welled in his eyes. He had done it again.

His sense of humor was dry and witty. You just never knew when he would come up with a crack that would send everyone reeling. What made his comments even more humorous was that basically he was a serious conservative guy. So it was especially funny when the joke happened to be on him. He was a very distinguished gentleman; a God-fearing, family man and an attorney. One day he was having breakfast at the Elks Club before catching the commuter train from suburban Des Plaines to downtown Chicago where he had a legal hearing later in the morning. Having dressed in a hurry before he left home that morning, he had not noticed that when he sat down on his valet to tie his shoes, my mother's bra, having been casually slung over the valet the night before, had attached itself to his black cashmere overcoat. So there he was, walking from the Elks Club to the train station, black coat with white bra flapping behind him in the breeze. As he later told the story, a very proper looking elderly couple came up to him and asked if he had enjoyed a nice night the evening before, and questioned whether perhaps he left in a bit of a hurry. Poor Dad. For the rest of his life, he never lived that story down.

Dad was pretty tenacious, too, and he taught me the virtue of perseverance. When I was about five, I decided it was time to take the training wheels off my green two wheel Husky bike. I was grown-up now, in school (kindergarten!) and wanted a ride that matched my newfound maturity. So dutifully, Dad removed the training wheels and walked and ran up and down the sidewalk in front of our house for days, holding on to the bike so that I wouldn't lose my balance. I don't know how many times we made that run up and down the block but it must have been hundreds. I would always lose control somewhere around the big elm tree at the edge of our lawn, very near the sidewalk. Frustrated, I decided to give up and told Dad to put the wheels back on. He told me he didn't have time until the following weekend. So, if I wanted to travel, I had no choice but to keep trying. Eventually, it happened. Success!!! All of a sudden, without even realizing it, I was sailing along, right past that elm tree and on toward the Venson's house on the corner. There I had to come to a screeching halt, because I wasn't allowed to cross the street. But I had done it. By myself. Dad made it inconvenient for me to give up, and of course, he had planned that all along.

He also got me through college. Not just financially, although he and my mother paid a king's ransom for a private school even when I had scholarships I did not use to other institutions. But I wanted to go to Cornell College in Iowa, and if I wanted Cornell, then that's what he wanted for me. I had done really well in high school, and figured college would also be a snap. I didn't count on homesickness, professors I didn't agree with (and who graded accordingly), adjusting to living with a roommate who was so totally worldly compared to my relative innocence, it was scary. She even smoked, for goodness sakes! So a whole two months into the college experience, I found myself with a D in my intended major of political science and on the phone in the hall closet to home. In those long ago days in 1966 we didn't have cell phones or even regular phones in our dorm rooms; there was a communal phone in the hallway that fifty girls shared. We had to go into the utility closet with the cord stretched to get any privacy. So there I sat, in the dark, wedged between the broom and dust mop and vacuum cleaner, sobbing across the long distance wires to my father. I was sure I was going to flunk out of school. I don't remember what he said; although it probably included the Bible verse, "let not your heart be troubled," because that was his mantra. But I do remember that he made me feel better, and gave me further resolve not to give up. With his encouragement, I went back to class the next day. I never did get an A from that professor, but I did end up passing the class with a B, and from then on, things were much easier.

Perseverance. Family. Humor. Music. Country. LEGACIES. Amazingly enough, they were all part of his final days. It was as if he was teaching us everything all over again. Dad fought his disease with uncommon courage and tenacity, and when he passed from this life the family that he held dear surrounded him. Before he died, he kept us all in stitches in the hospital with his wit and humor. The gospel music sung by my favorite group soothed me the days just preceding the funeral. The ceremony at the Veteran's Cemetery embodied all the patriotism and love of country that meant so much to him.

But now what? The day of the service, I only knew one thing. I didn't want to be a grown-up woman with grown-up children of my own. I wanted to be little again; I wanted my Daddy back. I wanted him to be able to teach me, to guide me, but mostly, I just wanted him to be there. As we left the restaurant where we had gone for lunch after the service, I saw something gleaming in the afternoon sun in the parking lot. A penny. My heart skipped a beat, for this bordered on the supernatural. Nearly twenty years earlier, after the death of my maternal grandfather, my mother and other family members began finding pennies in odd locations and at important crossroads in their lives. It had become family lore that Grandpa was still there, ever the patriarch, watching over us all and leaving those little copper reminders of his presence and his love. Now, the very day that we laid my father to rest, I found my first penny. Other family members were to find them as well in the days and weeks to come. We found them at graduations, when we landed new jobs, on birthdays, even on ordinary days when we just needed a lift.

In the years since his passing, I have accumulated several dollars in coins from Dad. Some were dimes and quarters and nickels (every time I find money somewhere, I assume it is from him and that the higher denominations are either attributed to inflation, or how badly I needed the encouragement). But the majority of my bounty is in pennies. Each one came at a time when I really needed to hear from Dad. I know now he will always be there for me and that he's still watching over me. What a legacy he has left us all.

17 HOLIDAY JOURNEY/THANKSGIVING DIARY

I think about families a lot at Thanksgiving, even more so than at Christmas. Maybe it's because Thanksgiving offers no incentive for being together except that elusive, mysterious tie that binds us together.

Erma Bombeck

Scott and me hosting a Thanksgiving dinner

T

he following is an excerpt from a journal I kept in the late 1990's. It has not been embellished.

I knew I should have been worried in late October when my daughter's boyfriend said he "might" be coming for Thanksgiving dinner at our house. "No problem," I told him, "just let me know about a week before so I can make necessary plans."

November 1. The Boyfriend is coming. That makes ten, a nice number. I go to the craft store to get cute things to make place cards. I am pleased.

November 3. Attend high school football game where niece is a cheerleader and sit next to college-age nephew. I remember what it was like when my daughters were in college and were alone or had "orphaned" friends for the holiday. I magnanimously tell nephew that he may bring a friend from school if he wants. I feel really proud of myself.

November 5. Boyfriend is not coming. We're back down to nine, but if my nephew brings a friend, we will have an even number again. No worries.

November 6. We have dinner with our best friends, Jack and Claudia. Their daughter and son-in-law will be with his parents for the holiday, and they are alone. No one should be alone on Thanksgiving, so I invite them and their grown son. That brings us to thirteen now, I think. It is time to go back to the craft store.

November 10. Boyfriend is coming. He has to work the next day, so can't make it all the way to his parents' home in Albuquerque and back in time. Sigh.

November 18. My sister calls. My nephew has invited two fraternity brothers. She has told him to un-invite someone, that I had only authorized ONE person. I say, "I would love to have both, but no way will my table accommodate fifteen." I feel bad, however, so I relent. "If they all don't mind sitting at a card table, they are welcome." Larger sigh.

November 18. (later in the day) My niece calls. She is seventeen; nephew's frat brothers are nineteen. She wants to sit at the card table, too. Wonderful. That at least gives us more room at the big table. I am trying to go with the flow. I'm proud of myself.

November 19. It is Sunday before the big day, and I'm getting ready to set the table. I ask my husband to put in both table leaves. He yanks on one side of table and the railings underneath break, wresting screws from the now splintered wood. The table collapses. My husband thinks he can fix it. Since his carpentry skills are close to non-existent, I suggest he call a professional, or at least our brother-in-law, who professes to know the difference between a hammer and a screwdriver. Husband resists my advice, and lies on his back under table for twenty minutes scratching his head. Next he reaches for the Yellow Pages. Sixty minutes and several hang-ups later, he relents and calls our brother-in-law. Another hour passes, and after much banging, screwing, expletives and glue, the table is fixed, they tell me. I am too stressed to set it.

November 20. I finally get to it. It is a major production. I pull out a special tablecloth, centerpiece, china, silver, crystal, and individual place cards especially hand crafted for all attendees. Every square inch of the table is covered with my very best, lovingly placed. The phone rings. My daughter asks, "Mom, did you set the table yet?" I don't want to ask why, but I am brave.

The Boyfriend is not coming again. He has decided to make the trip home after all. The noise I utter is no longer a sigh.

November 21. For some strange reason, call me crazy, I decide not to remove the Boyfriend's place setting. After all, there are still two days until Thanksgiving. At two minutes before five pm (just before the local TV station where she works is about to go on the air; requiring her attention in the studio), my daughter calls. She is smart enough to know that by calling with her tidings at this particular time, I will be pre-emoted from erupting for more than a few seconds. Boyfriend felt bad he canceled; he is coming after all. I congratulate myself on having the foresight to leave his plate on the table. Moving his place card next to mine, I work on my best glare.

November 22. It is time to start cooking. I pick up my mother and her dog, both of whom will be houseguests for two days. Mom can't walk or drive because of recent surgery. I cook some more. We pick our older daughter up at airport. This has been an easy day. There is only one cloud. We have a new dog, eight months old. He is a male. My mother's dog is a 3-year-old female. Both are neutered/spayed. It doesn't matter; they want to have sex. Tomorrow is going to be a long day.

November 23. THANKSGIVING. I wake up, read the paper, have a leisurely breakfast. The dogs are enjoying each other on the patio. My older daughter is stabbing the turkey with some big hypodermic needle. She says this will make it taste better. My husband is hovering and insisting that the meat thermometer goes in the breast. I don't think so. A discussion ensues. We look it up in a book, and consult Mother. We remove dogs from each other. I win, we move thermometer to the thigh. I finally get breakfast dishes done about noon. My husband decides to cook hamburgers for lunch, regardless of the fact that we have recently finished breakfast and guests will arrive in less than four hours for dinner. A discussion ensues again. He wins. I do more dishes. We separate the dogs. I think of reasons to send my husband to the store, many times. I tell my Mother that her dog cannot stay for dinner; we do not need a floor show. I solve the problem by taking the dog to my sister's house. Bless her! Relative calm ensues. I shower and dress for the company. They all show up.

Postscript: Of a twenty-three pound turkey, the three college boys consume approximately twenty-one pounds before it is even passed to the other guests. My best friend helps with the dishes and breaks an heirloom cup from my china service. The service is over one hundred years old and has been passed down three generations. I watch my Mother give my best friend The Look. My friend is crying. I am sick. (We later find a place that will repair the cup, so everyone feels better). The doorbell rings. Our friends' daughter and son-in-law are finished at his parents' house and decide to have dessert with us. What's a couple more? We actually have a pleasant couple of hours visiting before they all go home. The best news of all? My sister has Christmas.

18 LIFE JOURNEY/THE HOUSE TOUR

He is the happiest, be he king or peasant, who finds peace in his home.

Johan Wolfgang von Goethe

Just after moving into our first real house, Rolling Meadows, Il, 1974.

S
everal years ago after dinner with a celebrity friend, we were invited back to his home. As we drove past the friendly security guard, I noticed an enormous structure up on the hill.

"That must be a clubhouse," I remarked to my husband. "It's too big to be a house."

I was wrong; we were in California after all. The house belonged to our friends.

As they took us on a tour of their beautiful home, complete with custom finishes throughout, I noticed that every room had its own entertainment center with all the state of the art equipment of the day. I also noticed that every room's entertainment center had its own little adjacent room just for the cords. I never knew anyone that had cord rooms before.

As elaborate as the home was, it was most definitely a family home. One large passageway was covered from ceiling to floor with family portraits, and there was even one entire room devoted to family photo albums, lovingly catalogued. It occurred to me that my friend was not unlike most of us. He lived differently than most of us could ever dream, but the things that were important to him are central to us all. The tour of his home evoked a house tour of my own:

My tour begins in Evanston, Illinois, in an apartment. I recall nothing of the building itself except that it is three stories. I arrive here as an infant and leave at about age four. I get my thumb stuck in a water fountain at a nearby park when I am two. At Christmastime, I dance around the tree on my father's feet to a waltz, wearing a pretty red dress. It is happy here.

On a quiet street in a suburb called Park Ridge is a small ranch house, dark brown in color, with a detached garage and a big elm tree in the front yard. Across the street is Carpenter Elementary School. Here I learn to ride my bike, develop a crush on the next-door neighbor boy, and wear out the swing set in the back yard. I spend hours with my friends Janet, Caron, Laura, Jayney, Sandy, Diane, Cheri and Nancy. We are all in Brownies together, and my mother and Janet's mom are the troop leaders. In fall, we pick apples off our own tree. For some reason, they always taste better than the ones that come from the store. My tiny bedroom in the back of the house overlooks the yard. How I hate the black and white abstract checkered wallpaper. Why in the world would my mother choose that? But otherwise, I love my room. Our house is so small that I can eavesdrop on everything that goes on from the privacy of my bedroom. The laughter of my parents and their friends, my new baby sister crying in her bedroom right next to mine, my father playing "Goofus" on the organ in the living room, the sounds of my mother on the wall phone in the kitchen. I hear the neighbors next door arguing constantly. That makes my existence seem even more secure. From our living room, I squint at the little square black and white TV screen dwarfed by the enormous cabinetry that it is surrounded by. I don my coonskin cap for each episode of Davy Crockett, or perhaps my mouse ears for the Mickey Mouse Club. I grow into adolescence at this address, and experience my first taste of death when my beloved grandmother passes away. I start high school. It is the home I return to that dreary, cold November day when President Kennedy is shot. When I see my staunchly Republican mother weeping when I get home, somehow things don't seem so secure any more.

In 1964 my house tour takes us to the country. Dad is selling real estate surrounding a new golf course and country club. He thinks it will be better for business if we live there as well. So we leave the little house in Park Ridge behind and move into a custom built home on Cumberland Circle in Long Grove. On our very own lake! With a (small) beach! It is a multi-level house, and it is beautiful. The entryway opens into a huge living room with floor to ceiling windows overlooking the lake and golf course. A formal white brick fireplace takes up one entire wall. A circular staircase connects the two levels; each step sporting a different color carpeting (sixties chic). Downstairs is an enormous family room with a complete second kitchen and a mammoth stone fireplace. So many of life's passages take place in this house. My friend Janet from elementary school days and her family join our family as we watch Neil Armstrong land on the moon. Another event is my 16th birthday party. It is an ice skating party, in December, in Illinois. However, that weekend it is sixty-five degrees, in December, in Illinois. It is also my first boy-girl party, and it is a disaster. The lake is mush, the company awkward. Everyone leaves early. I hate being sixteen.

The following years speed by. There is Prom, then college, then a short stint in law school, where I meet my husband. I remember peering through the master bedroom window as he asks my father for my hand out in the garden. We celebrate with already iced champagne and impromptu tuna fish sandwiches. Then comes the Wedding Day, where the house is a flurry of friends, relatives and photographers.

The next stop on my tour is my first as a grown woman. It is a one-bedroom apartment in Palatine, Illinois, and it is our first home as a married couple. We are so proud fixing it up with second hand furniture, elbow grease and paint. Paint-by-number pictures adorn the walls. Laundry has to be carried upstairs to the pay machines. There is a little dog named Corky, who, distressed at being alone all day while we toil at work to buy him biscuits, systematically eats his way through the carpeting, right down to the concrete. When we vacate this apartment, we do NOT get our security deposit back!

There are incredible cooking disasters. When we married, my parents' friends were all fairly prosperous. Instead of the typical kitchen shower, I am blessed with a silver and crystal shower. This is all very marvelous, except I enter married life with few necessities, like cookware. This oversight becomes glaringly apparent when we host one of our first dinner parties for my husband's mother and young brother. I decide to make chicken, mostly because it is the only thing I know how to make. However, lacking a baking pan, I opt for the only thing I can find, which was a cookie sheet. Several minutes into the roasting process, the shrieking of the smoke alarm interrupts our cocktail conversation as the chicken grease starts splattering. My mother-in-law is sympathetic; my seven-year-old brother-in-law laughs his head off.

We also make a baby here, and being pregnant requires more room. Smaller than the house that I grew up in, our new house in Rolling Meadows is literally a box made of siding and shingles. It consists of a living room, kitchen, a family room extension with orange shag carpeting, two bedrooms, and detached garage. No extras. The furnace is in the hallway next to the bathroom, out in the open for all to see. Not exactly Park Avenue. At the time, however, it seems like a palace. We get our first taste of home ownership at this address, and it is not pretty. We decide to put in a new kitchen floor. I want red carpet tiles to match my poppy red appliances. It must be a throwback to that black and white room I had as a kid; I want bold color all around me. It is also the 70's and color is in. Only it is too hard to pull up the old floor, and we don't have the money to hire a professional, so we just leave it and lay the carpet tiles right over it. Big mistake, huge. The uneven floor cracks every time someone walks on it. Pieces come up in chunks for months. But it doesn't matter, because we are busy with our baby daughter and building a life.

Another pregnancy necessitates a larger house with more than two bedrooms. So next on my tour is the Chicago suburb of Lake Zurich, about fifty miles northwest of the city. There is no train for my husband to take to work downtown so his commute becomes longer, but the house is a pretty split level with a nice yard on a cul de sac. We have really terrific neighbors, and we are friends with them all. We feel like we are putting down roots. I take my daughter's hand in the driveway and walk her to the corner to catch the bus for her first day of kindergarten. I plan birthday parties, and referee sandbox sessions and bandage skinned knees. My husband teaches another generation how to ride a bike. When we start making some money and decide to upgrade, it is sad to leave. It is also hard to sell.

After 637 long days in a depressed real estate market, we finally sell the place and are able to buy a new home, a new stop on the tour. We move closer to the city again, to Arlington Heights. Both girls are in elementary school. I become a Brownie leader, just like my mother before me. We have hit the big time, although we don't fully appreciate it. The home is a striking two story white brick colonial with a full basement, four large bedrooms, huge kitchen, separate dining room, and a big back yard with lilac trees...my favorite. There is a Cadillac in the garage. The house also has baby blue carpeting. Most houses in the early 80's have beige or off-white or cream or ivory. Color is out in the 80's. I love blue, however, and the instant I see the carpeting I know the house is meant to be ours. It is nestled on a tranquil lane in an upscale suburb, and we love it.

This is the house of Brownies and Care Bears and Teddy Ruxpin. It is the house from which I buried the last two of my grandparents and where we return after our memorable New Years' Eve meeting with the Oak Ridge Boys.

We could have stayed here forever, but for the weather. Chicago's winters and lack of sunshine are just getting to be too much. I hate them and I want out. So after only three years, we make a colossal lifestyle decision and pull up all our roots to move cross-country to Arizona. We want to retire there before it was time to retire.

Although I have often felt that my husband could have stayed in Chicago forever and been perfectly content, to me Scottsdale Arizona is paradise. There are no lilac trees, but there are beautiful scarlet bougainvillea bushes. The sun almost always shines. The brutally searing summers seem a small price to pay for the eight months of idyllic weather. We throw out our heavy coats, our boots and our snow blower. It is our first adventure with building a new home, and it does not start well. Ours is the first house to be built on the street. The day they are to break ground, it snows. It never snows in Scottsdale, Arizona, but it does that day. I'm convinced this is because we are under a time limit to finish paperwork and move out of the old house. We learn a lot building. Rule number one is never be one thousand miles away when a house is being built. Before faxes, smart phones and texts, we have no way of noticing that the structure is set way too far back on the lot, giving us the back yard the size of a postage stamp. Our pool has to be redesigned to squeeze into the yard. Although it isn't as spacious as the Arlington Heights house, it is still roomy. To us it seems like we have our own little private resort. We are living our retirement dream well before our time.

This is the house of cheerleading and swim teams, boyfriends and proms, tantrums and tears, wounded hearts and stretching wings. The refrigerator door is a colorful array of magnets, holding team schedules and practices, football games and meetings, categorizing our lives. The house is crammed to the rafters with laughter and dirty socks and homework. Isn't it only a moment later that it is empty and quiet and neat, as first one child, then the other, leaves for college?

The quiet doesn't last too long though, because soon each of the girls brings home the man of her dreams. The house sees two weddings, and eventually the birth of five grandchildren. An office is converted into a playroom; a security fence goes up around the pool. It becomes "Grandma and Grandpa's house." It sees much joy and some sorrow as well. It is the house we leave a couple of times a year to travel all over the world, and is our welcoming haven upon each return. It is the house I come back to after burying both of my parents, years apart, but a little part of me dies with each of them. It is the house where my husband suffers a traumatic brain injury from which he almost recovers, but not quite.

I thought it was going to be the last house on my tour. I thought we would live here for a long time, maybe until it is time to discuss a "retirement community." But it is not to be. Even though my husband technically dies in a hospital, in reality, he dies here, in this home, in our bed. The house becomes too big for just me, and finances dictate that it has to be sold. Thirty-two years in one place is a long time, and it is gut wrenching to pack up and let it go. But the new owners are a young couple who want to start a family here, and that makes me very happy. My wish is that they experience everything we did, from first steps to proms, from skinned knees to weddings. They have a good house to live in, with a million stories in its walls.

As for me, I get lucky. I find a much smaller house just a short distance from my old one. It is only 1500 square feet, but it has a nice layout, a small yard for my dog, and three bedrooms so that I can have an office and a dedicated room for the grandkids. It also comes with fantastic neighbors, who have helped me rebuild my new life. It feels like home almost immediately, even if it doesn't have any cord rooms.

19 BASEBALL JOURNEY/SECTION 209

I think there are only three things America will be known for 2,000 years from now when they study this civilization: the Constitution, jazz music, and baseball.

Gerald Early

At one of my favorite places…the ballpark

W

hen it's winter in Arizona, I try not to complain. While the rest of the country is shivering and slipping and sliding and bundling up against subzero temperatures, I bask in southwest sunshine. On a bad day, the temperature hovers around sixty degrees. Yet, I am restless. This is a hard part of the year for me; halfway between the last baseball game of the season and the promise of spring training.

For as long as I can remember, I have loved baseball. My dad took me to my first games, at legendary Wrigley Field in Chicago. We would go only once or twice a year, but each game was an event. Mom rarely went with us, but she would fix us tuna sandwiches and add some fruit (she thought that ballpark food was bad for us). In the mid-fifties, when I was growing up, Dad would always be able to buy field box seats right at the ticket window the day of the game. We sat in row five or six, right behind the Cubs dugout, and enjoyed our day together. After a couple bites of sandwich, Dad would call over the hot dog vendor, followed by the ice cream vendor, and always the Cracker Jack vendor. He did not share Mom's qualms about ballpark food.

"It isn't a ballgame without a hot dog," he'd say.

From this vantage point, we witnessed Ernie Banks' 500th home run disappear over the ivy, and cheered Milt Pappas' no-hitter. Players and events are etched in my mind. Ron Santo and Andre Dawson and Ryne Sandberg. Rick "Groceries" Ruschell and Fergie Jenkins. The 1969 Collapse. (I have hated the Mets ever since). Lou Brock before he became a Cardinal and Greg Maddox before he became a Brave. This was Chicago baseball. These are the memories of a childhood. In those days we went to the park to enjoy baseball, the game. It was before salaries soared. It was before free agents and labor strikes. We didn't go to see prima donna stars; we came to see a ball game.

When the Diamondbacks franchise was awarded to my adopted new home in Phoenix, it was a cause for great celebration. I devoured every news item about the team, eagerly anticipating baseball in the desert. Seat selection day was akin to a trip to the best toy store in the world. I was so excited as we made the trek downtown, surveyed the mockup of the stadium and chose our seats. Section 209, Row 6, seats 7, 8, 9, 10. Diamond Infinity Level. Parking privileges in the adjacent garage. Arizona Baseball Club restaurant privileges. Private walkway to the stadium. Pretty fancy stuff, and a dream come true. I loved our seats. Our view from the second level between home plate and first base allowed us to see each play develop in its entirety. The line of sight was excellent. The "play within a play" became more apparent. From these seats we treated my Dad to a couple of baseball games before he passed away. What a thrill it was for me to be able to take him to a game! Even though he was on a restricted diet, we always indulged in a hot dog.

"It's not a baseball game without a hot dog, Dad!"

Section 209 had its regulars: Dan and Tina, who sat in front of us. Alberto, the psychiatrist, who high-fived us after each remarkable play. The lovely couple in the first row, she with the hat covered with pins and the score pad on which she recorded every game. There was Steve and little daughter Hayley, who reminded me of another father and daughter from two generations ago. And Joe and Audrie Garagiola, who had the seats right next to ours. What a joy it was getting to know them. Joe was forever entertaining our entire section with his wit and baseball knowledge. Audrie was always charming and gracious. During one game, a youngster, urged on by his father, asked Joe for his autograph. Not really knowing who this legend was, but told by his father Joe was someone famous, the child turned and asked with reverence,

"Did you play with Babe Ruth?"

The look on Joe's face was worth the price of admission.

There were many thrilling baseball moments in that sparkling new park, of course. Who could ever forget opening night, or the magical World Championship season? But one of my biggest baseball thrills came on a night when the players had not yet taken the field. It was the night of the first playoff game in 1999. There I was, standing next to Joe and Audrie, he with his arm around her shoulders, tears in his eyes, as the Western Division Championship flag was unfurled. Joe, Jr., Diamondbacks General Manager, stood beside him. The pride on Joe, Sr.'s face that extraordinary night was that of a father for his son, and it was awe-inspiring. This was baseball in its purest form, and this was a snapshot of America. Section 209 gave me the best of the best. We moved to section 208 a few years later, and held onto our season tickets for 19 years. I had to give them up after my husband passed away, and it broke my heart. But those memories of the crack of the bat, the cheers, the groans, and the magical moments will stay with me forever. Is it spring yet?

20 HISTORICAL JOURNEY/SEPTEMBER 11, 2001

Freedom is never more than one generation away from extinction. We didn't pass it to our children in the bloodstream. It must be fought for, protected, and handed on for them to do the same, or one day we will spend our sunset years telling our children and our children's children what it was once like in the United States where men were free.

Ronald Reagan

Flag found in rubble of World Trade Center

128

T

he first phone call of the day awakened us at 6:30 a.m. when our daughter Ginger told us to turn on the TV. By seven, Kristy had also called. Images on the screen were surreal. The Statue of Liberty's torch, framed against a background of billowing gray smoke, was first to penetrate the senses. Then the horror began to unfold. The planes diving into buildings, the fires, and the landscape changing in front of us, as the symbols of both capitalism and national security were destroyed. The screams we could only imagine from so many miles away. Fighter jets in the air and the National Guard in the streets.

The eye saw, but the brain couldn't comprehend. We worried about a relative who worked in New York and friends who were visiting. We watched our grim President resolutely striding back into the White House, having the impossible task of trying to reassure the nation, and it broke our hearts. Finally, we saw the shredded skin of a 110-story building, lying in ruins, in the shadow of a torn American flag still fluttering proudly in the dark night.

There were so many questions that couldn't be answered. Was there anybody in the United States who was not touched by this? How could this happen...and why? Would we ever feel really safe again? Fighting tears all day, I lost the battle when the normally bickering Congress stood united on the steps of the Capitol singing "God Bless America." Wherever we live, whoever we are, whatever our age or our beliefs, we were being tested that day. But with God's help, we would not only survive; we would be a better people. I believed that in my heart.

In the days that followed, I nested. I cooked and vacuumed and cleaned out closets, most of the time having one eye glued to the mind-boggling images on television. During a purge of a long forgotten closet, I came upon an essay I wrote back in 1966 when I was seventeen years old. It was entered in an American Legion contest, and I won first prize. I hadn't seen it or thought about it in decades. Now, as I sat cross-legged on the bedroom floor reading the yellowed, manually typewritten pages, I wept.

What Does the Flag Mean?

Johnny was watching the parade with his grandfather. He was only ten, so there were many things about which he didn't know. The day was Memorial Day, or Flag Day, or Independence Day. It didn't really matter. All Johnny knew was that there were bands playing, people marching, and lots of flags. He liked it. Suddenly, he became puzzled. "Grandpa," he asked, "what does our flag really mean? I know it's the American flag, and that we fly it on top of buildings, and they paint it on the space-crafts, but what does it stand for?"

Johnny's grandfather looked down fondly at his grandson and said,

"Well, Johnny, it's just about everything. You see those pretty colors there? Well the red – that's stands for courage. The courage of all Americans to fight for what they believe. It also symbolizes the blood of our soldiers who died protecting our freedoms.

That blue stands for loyalty, son. The loyalty of all Americans for their country. And the white – well the white means the purity or the goodness of the American people.

Do you understand, Johnny?"

"Uh-huh, Grandpa, I think so."

"But wait, Johnny, there's more — much, much more. That flag, that piece of bright-colored cloth symbolizes the history of the United States. It's the ringing of the Liberty Bell; it's a blacksmith fanning his fire. It's an Alexander Graham Bell or a Henry Ford or a Thomas Edison.

It's also a tramp on Maxwell Street in Chicago choosing to contribute nothing. It's a bunch of kids like you, Johnny, eating ice cream and hot dogs on the Fourth of July. It's church, home, and friends and relatives. It's San Francisco or Kalamazoo, Chicago or Timbuktu, Texas or Rhode Island. It's millionaire and beggar.

Oh, Johnny, it's so many things. You see in that flag, Johnny, all the generals you like to read about. Generals like York, Marshall, MacArthur, Eisenhower.

That flag is also battlegrounds, Johnny, and the brave soldiers who fought and died on them."

"You mean battles like Pearl Harbor and Normandy and Bataan, and maybe even Civil War battles? Stuff like that?"

"Yes, Johnny, you have the right idea."

"Gee, Grandpa, that's a lot of things. Is there anything else?"

"Oh, son, there are so many things that our American flag means to us. And there will be many thousands more. See how proudly it waves in the breeze? Well, Johnny, that flag is just bursting with pride just because of all the things that it is — and will be. As the years go by, son, as long as there is a United States of America, that flag waving in the sunlight will mean more

and more things and it will wave even more proudly than it is now."

"Golly, Grandpa, I never knew it was so much. Can I have one of them, please?"

Johnny's grandfather bought him a small flag and handed it to him.

"Take care of that, Johnny," he said. "That's your country you're holding in your hand."

"I know, Grandpa, but how do you really take care of a flag?"

Johnny's grandfather smiled down at him, and whispered, "Just think of all it means, Johnny, just think. Then you'll know. All you have to do is remember all

that it stands for, and you can't help but respect it with all your heart. Love it Johnny. Remember, you're a part of it, too."

"Yes, Grandpa. I think I understand."

Eighteen months later, I found myself at the American History Museum in Washington, D.C., just a short distance from where one of those planes had slammed into the side of the Pentagon. The museum had a special exhibit of artifacts recovered from the sites of the attack on our country. The first thing that struck me was an American Flag. It was torn and ragged and filthy. There were gaping holes in its middle section. Over one-fourth of its blue field had vanished, and only forty of its stars remained. It was recovered from a landfill in Staten Island, New York, dumped there with other debris from the World Trade Center. It was not very big. It had never flown from atop a building nor had it stood at attention in a lobby, for it was standard issue, much like the duplicates many of us fly from our homes everyday. Perhaps at one time it graced someone's office, or maybe a restaurant, or a shop. It was just one of millions manufactured by a factory somewhere.

But today it had a new home, and new neighbors. And it was special. Lovingly mounted and encased in glass, it was surrounded by a gleaming silver frame. A bright floodlight cast a glow upon it. It shared an unassuming room now at the Museum with other ordinary objects; objects that had now become extraordinary. There was the helmet and fire gear worn by FDNY Battalion Chief Joseph Pfeifer, the first fire chief to arrive at the World Trade Center on September 11. He lost his brother Kevin that day, another firefighter. Next to the uniform was the smashed, bent and burned door of a fire department truck. It was the only remaining remnant of the entire vehicle. Behind the door in the same case rested two steel girders, orange in color, twisted beyond recognition. Two airplane fragments lay next to them; one a window frame, clearly recognizable. I wondered who sat there and what he or she saw in the final seconds of life.

There was a crumpled, charred stairwell sign from the 102nd floor, and a fax machine so twisted and burned that you had to read the accompanying description to determine what it once was. I wondered how many souls died looking at that sign when all they had done was go to work that day?

There was a picture of the south tower, taken just before it collapsed. The photographer died seconds after it was taken. Did he know death was so close? There was a soot-covered briefcase, a singed wallet, shoes, and a doll. Did their owners survive? What horrors would they carry with them forever if they did?

There was a filing cabinet, determined to have come from a Ben and Jerry's ice cream store. Now twisted metal, it was about the size of a basketball. What happened to the people who might have been getting an early morning treat?

There was a television monitor recovered from the destroyed offices of the Navy Command Center at the Pentagon. It was only a frame with a big, black hole and dangling wires. Was someone watching the nightmare in New York on this television when the next plane hit Washington? There was a clump of coins, fused together by the intense heat. If this could happen to metal, it was incomprehensible to try to imagine what happened to humans.

There was a sign that directed visitors to the temporary memorial and crash site in a field in Pennsylvania. I wondered how many lives and what precious building those heroes saved from destruction?

There was a panel from the Wall of Prayers, a memorial to World Trade Center victims created at the entrance to Bellevue Hospital in New York. I remembered all those people holding pictures, talking to journalists, begging for information about their loved ones, and my heart broke all over again.

There was much more in this room. There were photographs, artifacts, and memorabilia of all kinds. Every bit of it wrenched the heart and brought tears. Yet it was also strangely reassuring to know that no matter where you were in the room, the ragged piece of cloth resting in its case, bathed in its light, watched over everything. Even though it was not big, it could be seen from every display case. It provided, even in its shabby state, a sense of comfort and pride, and yes, defiance.

My family accompanied me to the museum that day, and we all agreed that every American should be required to see this display. Every American should feel the pain, again. We were at war then, and still are, and every American should remember why. We did not start this war; others did. Those people and their sympathizers still want to destroy us and our freedoms. We must always remember that. The flag that I wrote about all those years ago now means more than it ever did. More courage, more loyalty, more battlefields, more soldiers, more resolve. God Bless America.

21 LIFE JOURNEY/IT WAS NOT JUST A BALLGAME

The one constant through all the years has been baseball. America has rolled by like an army of steamrollers. It's been erased like a blackboard, rebuilt, and erased again. But baseball has marked the time. This field, this game, is a part of our past. It reminds us of all that once was good, and what could be again.

James Earl Jones, Field of Dreams (1989)

With daughter Kristy at Game 7 of the 2001 World Series

I t was a balmy November night in the desert; the early evening dusk feathered by a few billowing clouds. The roar of the B2 stealth bomber preceded its jet-black silhouette, as it screamed above the stadium, its wingspan seemingly engulfing the cavity created by the retractable roof. Strains of a trumpet filled the night air, only to be replaced by pulsating music and the shrieks of fifty thousand souls. White pom poms resembled popcorn balls marching in perfect cadence throughout the ballpark. Illumination from the worldwide television equipment competed with the stadium lights. The aroma of hot dogs and cotton candy merged with the scent of burritos and beer, and mixed with the smell of peanuts and Cracker Jack. Together, it was a kaleidoscope for the senses.

It was also a dream. It was the dream of a little girl who went to her first baseball game in 1955 with her father, but had never witnessed anything like this. Now a grown woman, she gazed to the heavens several times that night, somehow trying to share the moment with the dad who was no longer here. There were thousands of stories as compelling as hers, thousands of people whose dreams were represented in that ballpark on that night. It was the dream of so many players who had toiled their whole careers for this grasp at immortality, but had never had an opportunity to experience the thrill of playing for the ultimate prize. They had been called too old, yet here they were, playing a boys' game. Now they were referred to as "mature veterans." And it was the dream of an Italian businessman from Chicago, who had assembled a sports conglomerate and redefined a city, creating new businesses and jobs and civic pride in the process. But in thirty-five years in professional sports, he had never won a major championship.

All of them had come together on one magical night, with one impossible dream. The dream was the glue that brought a community together. People with long allegiances to other cities and other teams now could call this one their own. A new generation of fans was christened that night; children who would carry memories of this event throughout their lifetimes and pass them on to their sons and daughters. Little girls sported glittery face paint and ponytails tied with purple ribbons; little boys wore caps on heads not yet large enough to fill them, proudly sporting the team's insignia. Miniature team jerseys adorned their backs. They heard the cheers, they felt the excitement, and they took a photograph with their minds. They were the future of the franchise.

And it was so many of life's lessons. It was gutsy performances by two men whose arms were about to fall off, but who dug deep down inside themselves to find something extra to give when it mattered the most. It was never giving up, no matter how bleak the situation appeared to be. Those lessons could not have been lost on a young Korean, whose wistful expression as he watched events transpire on the field, betrayed what he had learned just a few days before: that it is hard to perform under pressure, and that mistakes can bring agony. This young man had most certainly also learned a valuable lesson about friendship and team spirit from one of those "mature veterans," one who had waited his entire life for this experience. Just as glory was within his grasp, he watched it disappear on the wings of a baseball into a dark cold night, a baseball thrown by the young Korean. In a gesture of incredible compassion, his first reaction was to envelop his young teammate in his arms, in a public display of encouragement and empathy. His actions that bitter night spoke volumes, not only to the youngster, but also to the world.

It was also a diversion. And it was salve for the soul of a nation, a nation that had been severely wounded, physically and emotionally. It desperately needed reassurance that America's quintessential game, and by extension, its way of life, would go on, despite the heartache and sorrow, despite the unspeakable cruelty and horror. The symbolism was palpable; the drama indescribable. One team was steeped in tradition, the other an upstart newcomer. For seven nights in autumn, the balance had swung, first to one side, then the other. When it looked most hopeless, victory was seized from defeat, like a phoenix rising from the ashes. Not once, but several times. For both sides. Although the participants were battling each other, they were performing for the world. They were illustrating their resiliency, their steadfastness and their ability to overcome all obstacles. They were proving that hope is eternal.

It was a microcosm of an entire season. It had started off with the tantalizing promise of victory, but met with agonizing struggles and adversity, seeming to lurch toward a finish. There were times when defeat seemed certain. By the 7th inning winds were whipping the stadium, and the rain that began to fall in the desert was a metaphor for the doom sensed by the entire crowd. In the stands, the grown up little girl sat with her daughter, and tried not to let the heartbreak show. The Italian businessman sat slumped in his seat holding his wife's hand. His family surrounded him, as if to weave a cocoon around him and shield him from the impending pain. Only the players seemed focused. They were the 2001 version of "The Little Engine That Could." In the bottom of the 9th inning, behind 2-1, they came out of the dugout, one by one, like mighty gladiators. They marched into the arena and into the spotlight, and one after the other, with determination in their eyes and resolve in their hearts, slowly, tantalizingly, climbed a mountain and brought hope back. They brought it back to a little girl, back to an Italian businessman, back to a city, and back to a country.

Finally, in a miraculous finale, there was such sweet victory, such unrestrained joy. It almost happened as if in slow motion, so that it could be remembered in every detail for the ages. The screams of the multitudes faded into one sustained distant rumble. "We Are the Champions" blared from the loudspeakers. The field was a blur of flashbulbs and white uniforms. Strangers hugged strangers. The night sky, now clearing, was punctuated by purple fireworks. Car horns bleated throughout the city streets while a town found its place in the annals of sport. The little girl and thousands of others like her, the players and the Italian businessman had all waited a lifetime for this moment. And it was a moment that would last a lifetime. It was definitely not just a ballgame.

The two pitchers were Randy Johnson and Curt Schilling, the young Korean Byung Hyun Kim, the mature veteran Mark Grace, and the Italian businessman Jerry Colangelo, owner of the Diamondbacks. The teams were the New York Yankees and the Arizona Diamondbacks. It was the seventh game of the 2001 World Series. The little girl was me.

22 LIFE (AND DEATH) JOURNEY/GEORGE

No evil can happen to a good man, either in life or after death.

Plato

George and Phyllis with sons Jeff and Greg, 1984

"I have bad news. George has died." The voice on the other end of the phone belonged to my longtime friend, Phyllis, and the moment I heard her speak, I knew what she was going to say. We first met George and Phyllis in the early 70's when we were young married couples just beginning our families. My husband loved four-part harmony, and had joined a barbershop chorus in Arlington Heights, Illinois, called the Arlingtones. George was also in that chorus. Although most of the singers were decades older, there was a group of us, all in our late twenties or early thirties, who gravitated toward one another. Because George and Scott were youthful and agile, they were always in the front row for chorus performances and competitions. The rest of the chorus just sang; the front row had the moves. Soon, all the wives became friends as well. What fun we all had! We traveled to competitions together, we socialized, we raised our children together; we were inseparable.

There are barbershop choruses all over the country, and all were members of S.P.E.B.Q.S.A., or the Society for the Preservation and Encouragement of Barbershop Quartet Singing in America (now called the Barbershop Harmony Society). Each state or region had local competitions throughout the course of the year. The regional winners then met for an International competition annually, usually in July. The first International competition we ever attended was in 1976, in San Francisco. This was a big deal to a bunch of young kids, most of whom had never been west of the Mississippi. We flew out on a chartered plane to the west coast, reveling all the way across the country. Our little group within the chorus consisted of J.P and Diana, Steve and Linda, Kathy and Bob,

Bill and Shirley, George and Phyllis, and Scott and me. J.P. was a comical looking little Frenchman, with a handlebar mustache, slight of frame, who always dressed flamboyantly. Diana was a sweet, unassuming, trusting elementary school teacher, originally from Indiana. Steve was tall and handsome, a salesman for Sears with a wonderful sense of humor; Linda, a petite brunette with an infectious laugh who sometimes worked part time, but who mostly stayed home and raised their two boys. Kathy was a blonde with a terrific personality; and Bob was one of the most attractive men I had ever known, even though his hair was almost white by the time he was thirty-five. Bill was my boss at the law firm where I worked. He had two bad hips that had been surgically replaced; however, his physical impediment was completely overshadowed by his effervescent personality. His wife Shirley was a chain smoker, who tried to quit at least twice a year. Both were about fifteen years older than the rest of us, and they were sort of like the den parents. They had more money than any of us at the time, so the parties were always at their house; their rooms on our trips were always larger, and they paid for a lot of the alcohol. They were great den parents.

Then there was George and Phyllis. George was slightly balding, even as a young man, but what I noticed instead was the way his eyes danced. He was always laughing, always ready to play the practical joke, always attentive to everyone around him. He was also somewhat of a ladies man, and made every woman in the room feel like she was his favorite. Phyllis was a tall, striking woman, who had the most beautiful brunette hair. I was always envious, because it never seemed to wilt in the Midwest humidity like my limp strands did. She could sometimes have a sharp tongue, but she was a lot of fun, and became a good friend. A gathering was just not a party if any one from the group was missing.

While we were in San Francisco, we took in all the sights. We rode the trolley cars and strolled Fisherman's Wharf and visited Muir Woods. At night it was time for the singing. Competition went on all week, and winners were announced on Saturday night. The Arlingtones placed fifth that week, and that was cause for great celebration and camaraderie. It was with some alarm then that we discovered at one point just after midnight that J.P. was no longer among us. As the time passed, and Diana getting more concerned by the minute, Scott and George decided to go out to look for him. George had observed that J.P. had not treated Diana properly that whole week, and he theorized maybe he had disappeared to a bar to drown his sorrows, or even worse, look for some girl to pick up. So, the two guys meandered through the streets of San Francisco for hours, poking their heads into every bar and club and strip joint they could find. They returned to the hotel empty-handed and by this time Diana was frantic. As she was trying to decide whether or not to call the police, J.P ambled off the elevator, as nonchalant as could be. Last seen in the elevator heading to their room, the look on Diana's face indicated J.P. would not be getting much rest that night. Several years later, J.P. and Diana divorced, when he finally confessed he was gay. Shortly afterwards at a group dinner, George dryly commented,

"All those hours we looked for him, and we were just looking for love in all the wrong places!"

Our relationship expanded past barber shopping as well. For several years we would gather on Father's Day. George, Scott and either J.P. or Bob would play golf in the afternoon, while Bill drove the cart. Admission to the Father's Day tournament was either beer, Scotch or Crown Royal. The wives would assemble the kids

144

and we'd all congregate for an evening barbecue. One outing was particularly memorable. George lost one of his golf balls in the lake and proceeded to try to fish it out. He lost his footing (no doubt impeded by a combination of Crown Royal and Bud Light), and tumbled into the lake. All his friends stood on the banks, laughing hysterically. The only problem was that George got trapped in the mud and was rapidly losing his footing and sinking. The more he tried to convey his stress, the more his buddies laughed. They finally did extend a golf club out to him to grasp, but his hands slipped right off. This caused more amusement. Meanwhile, he continued sinking, until finally he was up to his chest in the muck. At this point, his comrades realized he might actually be in a predicament. Bill was dispatched in the cart to fetch a rope from the clubhouse. During his absence, the guys tried to keep George's spirits raised by offering him some, umm, spirits. Bill finally returned, the rope was secured around George's armpits and tied to the cart. Bill drove, the others pulled, and George popped out of the lake like a cork, caked in mud. Everyone assumed that the golf outing for the day was over; George however, insisted on finishing the round. He must have been winning.

George and Phyllis were the first to break up the gang when his job transferred him to Tucson, Arizona. The move hit me like a sledgehammer. First of all, they were breaking up the group; secondly, I was the one that had wanted to move there for years, not them. To me, Arizona was paradise. To Phyllis, it was a great big dust bowl with reptiles. I'm not sure she ever really changed her mind. They were sent off with a round of parties, tears, hugs, and promises to keep in touch.

There was no barbershop chorus in Tucson for George, so for a long time he made the four hour round trip drive to Phoenix to sing with the Phoenician chorus. One year later, when my husband was fortunate to pass the Arizona bar exam, we were able to follow them to the desert. As much as George tried, he could not convince Scott to join him in the chorus. That part of our life had ended. However, we did maintain the friendship for several more years, traveling back and forth on Interstate 10, visiting each other, having margarita parties by the pool, playing with the kids, ever so gracefully slipping into our forties. Then in 1990, George accepted a new position in Ohio. For all the reasons that seemed so good at the time, but meant nothing later, we never saw them again. Oh, we kept in touch; we called occasionally, we never failed to exchange Christmas cards with long notes. I knew George had found another chorus to join in Ohio, and I knew they still went to the international conventions every year, for barber shopping was his passion. Even after all these years, he was still in the front row. But although we remained in contact, we never did make the extra effort to see one another.

For me, it wasn't a relationship that I felt we needed to work on. We were such good friends that even though distance separated us, I knew there would always be a time that we would get together again. We had been apart before, and I knew when we finally did manage to meet up, the years would melt away and it would seem like last week since we had seen each other.

When we didn't get our annual Christmas card from them that year, I got that funny feeling that something might not be right. But I didn't pursue it; I just chalked it up to Phyllis being busy. I knew she was selling real estate; it was probably taking up all her spare time during a busy holiday season. So I let it go. I knew there would be time to chat again. Then I got the phone call. It was just a message on my machine. "Hi, it's Phyllis. I know we haven't talked in awhile, but please call me when you get a chance." My blood ran cold. I sensed this was not going to be a happy phone call. I called her, got her machine. I waited all day, playing out in my mind what could be wrong. The first thing I thought of was that George had died, but I immediately forced that out of my brain, and by late afternoon had decided that they were calling to tell us they were coming to Arizona for that long-awaited reunion. When my original fears were confirmed, and Phyllis described the last ten months of hell they had gone through, I was devastated. George was diagnosed with a brain tumor in June; by October he was in a nursing home and by April he was dead. He was fifty-nine years old. They didn't tell us earlier because he didn't want us to know; he wanted us to remember him as he had been.

I loved George. I loved his laugh and his crazy jokes; I loved his hugs and the way he danced with me. I loved the way he made me feel beautiful. I loved the twinkle in his eye when he teased me, which was often. I loved to watch him with his children, who he adored. I loved the way he loved his wife. I loved the time we spent together as young couples. And I loved the idea that there would be a time we would all be able to reminisce and relive those days. Time to have one more of those famous margarita parties or family cookouts or golf outings. But it was not to be. Because George was dead. And my heart hurt. He was the first of us to die. I've lost both my parents, and the passing of an older generation always brings with it a sense of your own mortality. But losing a contemporary brings it home with a wrenching kick in the gut. With this newfound grasp of the inevitability of death came an overwhelming desire to live life. I doubted I would ever feel the need to go bungee jumping or running with the bulls in Pamplona. However, I vowed to gaze a little longer at a sunset, hug my kids and grandkids a little more often, and never take a friendship for granted again.

Since George's death, Bob and Kathy divorced, and both remarried. J.P. disappeared somewhere in California; Diana remarried a wonderful man, lived in Huntington Beach, California for a long time, and recently moved to Michigan. She never had children, but she is godmother to my youngest daughter. Steve and Linda retired to Iowa to dote on their grandchildren. Shirley and Bill also both passed away, one of cancer, the other of liver disease. My husband is gone now too, and so is Phyllis, another victim of cancer. Life marches on, sometimes in ways we never expect.

The very next day after I found out George had died, I called Diana in California, and then I called Steve and Linda in Illinois. We talked and laughed and reminisced, and we realized we have something worth preserving. We realized that George brought us all together again, and we know he's up there planning that next golf outing or organizing the next barbershop show, waiting patiently for us all. What a great margarita party we will all have then. But for now, I miss you, George.

23 PARENTING JOURNEY/NEW HORIZONS

Nothing endures but change.

Heraclitus

The family in 2004

I woke up one morning and decided life was good. I had a stable marriage, two great kids, a comfortable home, and a terrific dog. My mother was healthy and active, my sister was my neighbor, and we enjoyed a varied social life with interesting friends. I had survived a year of deep depression, and I had actually come to covet my empty nest. Scott and I could pretty much do what we pleased. We could go to movies with our best friends at a moment's notice without worrying whether it was someone's dinnertime or whether it was our turn to pick up a gang from practice. We had two cars in the garage at our disposal whenever we needed them. We could indulge our love of baseball by buying season tickets and going to games three times a week. We could travel where we wanted and at the time of year we wanted. We had worked hard and were starting to reap the rewards.

Just as we had settled in to this satisfying existence, my kids decided to stir it all up a bit. I think it was their mission in life to not let us get in a rut and become boring middle-aged people. We first noticed that our lives were about to change when our youngest daughter invited us to have dinner with her boyfriend's parents. This could only mean their relationship was serious. We knew Martin quite well (he was the boyfriend that couldn't quite make up his mind about Thanksgiving a few years back), and we loved him. Still, this reality of a possible impending union seemed surreal. Was this all really happening? What made it all the more stressful was that he was about to change jobs, and move to Virginia for FBI training. Kristy announced that she had every intention of going with him, and that is when the world started spinning out of control. We didn't say much, but we did let her know that we thought it was insanity for her to quit her job, give up her car and apartment and travel across the country to live with a man who had not yet made her any kind of commitment. Well, maybe we did say enough so our opinion could not be mistaken. Fortunately, although she never said she verbally agreed with us, she apparently made her feelings known to Martin. On the day after Thanksgiving (that holiday seemed to tie us all together forever somehow), he called Scott to ask for our blessing. Tipped off by our daughter that this call was coming, my husband practiced his speech for days. He was going to let Martin sweat a bit, not because we didn't want him as a son-in-law, but because he thought it would be diabolically fun. When the call came, I was anticipating hearing lectures about finances, advice about credit cards, helpful tidbits about undying love and the like. Instead, all I heard from my perch on the couch was, "Hi, Martin. Uh-huh. Great. Wonderful. So, how's the weather out there?"

With that, Martin became an official member of the family. It took the dear boy two more months to actually make the proposal, and the wedding date was set for the following January, a year hence. At that point, Wedding Central finally went into action. I was prepared for this, however, because I had been practicing and planning for years. Whenever I went to a wedding of the daughter or son of one of my friends, I couldn't help but collect the little souvenirs, make note of what I liked and what I didn't like, think of how lovely the ice sculpture was, and pocket the business card of the DJ or the bandleader. If the dictum "anticipation is half the fun," was true, then I had been having the time of my life for years.

My husband thought I was nuts. As the father of two girls, he had dreaded the inevitable for as long as I could remember. "W" Day could never come too late for him. Not only were both girls the apple of his eye, and any guy they introduced to him met with a wary side-glance and much scrutiny, he turned a deaf ear when it came to wedding discussions. Instead he teased, "If it's this year, its hot dogs in the back yard; in another year, maybe we can move inside; we're looking at least ten years down the road if you want music from other than the stereo." His least favorite movie in the whole world was "Father of the Bride", either version.

Of course, this was his way of not dealing with The Day. If he ignored it long enough, maybe it would go away, and maybe his little girls wouldn't leave him for someone else. Maybe he could still buy those chocolate hearts on Valentine's Day, as he had been doing since they were small children, or maybe he could still grill them huge steaks on Sundays or chat about the Suns or who to pick in the Final Four.

So, for a long time we found ourselves in limbo. I was squirreling away pictures of wedding dresses; he was wondering (when he thought about it at all) if it would look too tacky to do a barbecue for the wedding dinner. Now that the real planning was actually upon us, I dove into it with frenzy. Kristy had moved to Virginia to be with Martin the spring before the wedding leaving us with her two cats (she was flying out and couldn't take them both with her on the plane.) We already had a dog. What were a couple more little furry things? Empty nests were over-rated anyway. With Kristy gone, we had to rely on email and digital cameras to communicate all our ideas to each other. As it was 2003, electronic devices were yet to be mainstream. Since the wedding was to be in Phoenix, I did the legwork at my end; she planned color schemes, bridesmaids' gowns, invitations, menus, guest baskets and decorations from her end. It was exhausting, and I was glad that by this time I had my part time travel agency business based out of my house, giving me the freedom to plan the wedding unless rudely interrupted by work. We made lists of our lists, and were so unbelievably organized it was frightening. My husband took the role my father had taken over thirty years before and wrote checks. It was his highest and best use. On the rare occasion when we asked for his opinion, he still tried to convince us about the possibility of hot dogs in the back yard. I gave him one job to do about six months prior to the wedding: to make a CD of wedding songs to play at our house while everyone was getting ready and to make a backup CD of the songs the DJ would play at the reception. He completed this task the day before the wedding.

At the other end of the country, Kristy and Martin's second bedroom, which had formally been the "man room", (that is, it contained all of Martin's old furniture that Kristy did not care for), had been transformed into the wedding room, otherwise known as Crafters Corner. Burgundy and silver ribbon filled the room from one end to the other, punctuated by stockpiles of vellum, glue, scissors, cardstock, silk roses and Styrofoam wreaths. Despite the chaos, everything was humming along smoothly. Kristy made a trip home in May and had planned others for August and October and December to take care of those details that only brides can do. The days and nights were filled to the brim, but we were coping, with both our timeline, and our ever-growing pile of "wedding stuff." The dog and two cats were mostly getting along, even though the dog scared the biggest cat silly causing him to spend his days hidden under a bed.

With about eight months to go before the big day, we got a call from our oldest daughter in Texas.

"Mom, Dad, guess what? I'm coming home."

"Terrific, honey, for a visit? When?"

I was silently calculating whether she would be here at the same time as her sister might be coming to visit.

"No, I'm coming home for good. I think I have a job with the Arizona Republic. If all goes well, I will start in August. Can I stay with you for a couple of months while I figure out where I want to live and buy a house?"

I could not speak for the tears that started flowing immediately. Ginger had been far away from us for eleven years, and it would be wonderful to have her home again. I cried some more when I realized that she would not be arriving alone. She would be adding her dog and her cat to our menagerie. If you're counting, that now made two parents, two adult daughters, two dogs and three cats under one roof.

"Of course you can stay with us for as long as you need to!"

Empty nest? What empty nest? She arrived the second week of August and moved into her old room. Her dog immediately tried to chase Kristy's two cats and just as immediately made fast friends with our dog. They were such good friends that they soon made up their own game of tug of war. I think they would have preferred to use one of the cats for this game, but we made them use a rag toy. Ginger's cat, however, did not like Kristy's felines, nor did he like our dog. Try as we did to acclimate everybody gradually, it was mass chaos. Our dog decided to play with Ginger's cat by chasing him; the cat hissed and dove under the bed, only to find Kristy's cat already hiding there. That of course resulted in a catfight of mammoth proportions. All animals were soon separated for good, except the two dogs, who were still usually playing tug of war. Along with all the wedding stuff all over the house, I now had three litter boxes in various rooms. I went to the store and bought some air fresheners.

Before long, Ginger had settled in at work and begun the search for her first house. She hired a real estate agent who looked to me like she had just graduated from high school. Very sweet girl, but I was not so sure about her expertise. My husband and I decided to take some time and go out house hunting with them. Ever impulsive and eager, Ginger decided she wanted to buy the first house she saw. It was a nice house, but we warned her that there were plenty of others out there, and we convinced her to look around a little more. After a weekend stomping about in the brutal Arizona August heat, she decided she still wanted to make an offer on the first house. Unfortunately, it had sold. Her teenage real estate agent warned us that it was a sellers' market and that homes went quickly. In other words, "Shut up, parents!" Perhaps she knew a little more than her youthful looks indicated.

In the next six weeks, we must have visited at least one hundred homes in the Phoenix metropolitan area. There was the weekend Ginger was enamored with older homes with character. That was fair enough, except the ones that were in her price range were not in very nice areas. There were homes in nice areas that should have been condemned. She made offers on at least three houses that sold before the ink on the contract was dry, but finally had an offer accepted only to lose the house when the owners refused to make corrections indicated by the inspection. She was getting frustrated and so were we, for her. She was tired of living back at home like a teenager. The cat was still under her bed, and the dogs' gums were tired from tug of war. The low point was one perfectly awful, miserably hot and humid Sunday that we spent looking at houses all day, then waited in line for an hour at a gas station. In the middle of summer a pipeline providing gas to the Phoenix area had burst, causing a gas shortage. Fueled by the media, lines resembled those nationwide during the late seventies. This was not the exciting fun-filled experience that buying a first home was supposed to be. However, all good things come to those who wait, or to use my father's mantra, "let not your heart be troubled." Just when she (and we) thought she would be living with us through eternity, a house came on the market. It was only two years old, in perfect condition, in a decent neighborhood only five miles away from us, AND it had a hot tub! This time, she put in an offer right away and got the house. Moving day was scheduled for the first weekend in November, and we were thrilled for her. The move went without incident, even though it ended up coinciding with the same weekend Kristy had her bridal shower. Why not cram a weekend with two big events, instead of just one?

Kristy eventually removed her cats; one each on two of her visits home, although Ginger's cat never came out from under the bed until moving day. The wedding went off with only a few minor hitches that nobody really noticed, or so they were kind enough to say. We got a wonderful new son in the process. Both of our beautiful daughters started new lives and were looking forward to new horizons. Our one-year hiatus from the empty nest was stressful, hectic, crazy, frenzied, demanding, and hilarious. It's a memory I wouldn't trade for anything.

24 PRIVILEGED JOURNEY/MR. PRESIDENT

Sometimes I wake at night in the White House and rub my eyes and wonder if it is not all a Dream

Grover Cleveland

With President George W. Bush in the Oval Office, November 2008

Just like Grover Cleveland, I wondered if it was all a dream as well. It was late October 2008, and I was up to my ears in wedding preparations, this time for our oldest daughter's impending nuptials in early November, when a phone call from my younger daughter interrupted me.

"Hi, Mom. You'll never guess. I have some good news and some bad news."

"What's that?" I nervously asked. Good news and bad news could never really be good.

"The President is inviting senior staff members to the White House for a formal photo op. The good news is that I can bring three people. So you and dad are invited to come with me and Martin."

"That's incredible news" I practically squealed, already thinking about what I would wear.

"But what's the bad news?"

"Well, the invitation is for November 5th, four days before Ginger's wedding."

Silence. How in the world was I going to make this work? We lived in Arizona, 2300 miles away from Washington, DC. November 5th was a Wednesday; we had the rehearsal dinner, bridesmaid parties and a Sunday wedding that coming weekend.

But for my husband and me, it was also a no brainer. Our daughter had worked for the President for the last two years as one of the press secretaries to a cabinet level officer. As a result we had been privileged to attend a Marine One landing, White House Christmas parties and Fourth of July events on the South Lawn. Each event had been very special, but we had never actually MET the President.

I immediately went into full travel agent and event planner mode, first calling my daughter the bride to ask if she minded us making a cross-country trip just days before the wedding.

"No, of course not" she graciously replied. "This is a once in a lifetime opportunity." And then "Um, you will be back in time, right?"

After assuring her that of course we would be back in plenty of time, I made plane reservations. We were to fly out to DC on Tuesday, Election Day, right after voting. We would spend the night at our daughter and son-in-law's house, go to the White House together, then all fly back to Phoenix late Wednesday afternoon. My daughter and her husband already had their plane tickets as they were coming in for the wedding.

Everything went according to plan until my daughter got a message from the White House early Wednesday morning that our time slot had been changed from noon until later in the afternoon. That meant we would miss our flight back to Phoenix. Scrambling, I changed all four of our tickets to Thursday morning - at great expense. I figured that with the time change in our favor, unless there was a major flight delay we would still make it back in time for a planned wedding event that night.

At the appointed hour, we made our way to the White House, went through security and were ushered in to the Roosevelt Room, a conference room just across the hall from the Oval Office. We waited our turn with several other communications staffers and their families. One by one, each family was called to go across the hall to meet the President. When it was our turn, an aide opened the door leading from the Roosevelt Room and we found ourselves in a hallway across from the large door leading to the most powerful office on earth. A solitary Secret Service agent stood guard at one side of the door.

The aide instructed us, "Now when the door opens, simply step forward and just go right on in."

I responded, "Okay, but all of a sudden, I am really nervous."

The Secret Service Agent cracked a slight smile and winked. We stood there for a couple of moments, although it seemed much longer. Suddenly the door swung open. Expecting another aide to be on the other side, I was astonished when President George W. Bush stood there at the door, gestured to us, and heartily said, "Kristy, Welcome! Come in and introduce me to the family."

Here was our little family in the Oval Office alone with the President of the United States, but for two staffers and a photographer! After handshakes all around and some small talk, there was a short policy discussion between the President and my daughter. I know I stood there with my mouth open listening to my youngest child discuss policy with the President of the United States! The President also complimented my son-in-law on his physique and told him he could tell he worked out. He thanked my husband and me for allowing our daughter to serve her country. We posed for a formal picture in front of the President's desk, engaged in a few more pleasantries, and then were discreetly ushered out through the Rose Garden to make room for the next family.

I doubt we were in the Oval Office more than ten minutes, and because of the plane change, it was the most expensive photo opportunity ever. But the experience was worth every penny. Meeting the President of the United States in the Oval Office of the White House is a privilege accorded to few. It was made even more special by the graciousness of the man himself, who on the day after an election where his party suffered a loss, only was concerned about thanking his staff and their families for the work they had done for him over the years. George W. Bush is a kind,

lovely man and a class act. It was my honor to meet him. And we had excellent cocktail stories to tell at the wedding reception.

25 TOGETHERNESS JOURNEY/THE FAMILY VACATION

Never get so busy making a living that you forget to make a life.

Dolly Parton

Family on vacation in the British Isles, 2009

A nd so it came to pass that with a newly minted married daughter and another son-in-law we already loved, my husband and I decided it might be fun to take a family vacation before the patter of little feet made that impossible for several years. My younger daughter had just announced she was expecting our first grandchild, so we decided to take the plunge as soon as possible, and we figured it would be a good way to get to know our new son in law, Jim, a little better. Being cruise aficionados, we thought a lovely ship experience would be a treat for the young adults, and afford us all a comfortable means to see a slice of the world. I was particularly anxious to return to the Normandy area of France, not only because it is one of my favorite places on earth, but also because I strongly believed the younger generation should see the beaches of World War II from somewhere else than a dry history book.

We chose Princess Cruises because they featured an itinerary to Great Britain and Northern France. It appealed to multi-generations, and we could also afford it. Passports were updated and visions of pubs, castles and the Beatles danced in our heads. We decided to meet in London, stay overnight for a couple of days to combat jet lag, then proceed to Southampton to meet up with the ship and begin our adventure.

The adventure decided to begin for us at the Phoenix airport. Upon arrival, we were met with the dreaded "delayed" sign when we got to our gate. We were connecting through Houston, and apparently they were experiencing a thunderstorm. Apologies to my friends in Texas, but doesn't Houston regularly experience thunderstorms? Nevertheless, this one seemed to be serious enough to delay the flight coming IN from Houston, which was our flight flying back out TO Houston. As we had over a two-hour connection before our flight to London, I wasn't too worried - at first. With each subsequent posting of yet another delay, I started to panic a little. Yes, we had two days in London, so missing the ship was not going to be an issue, but we had tickets to "Phantom of the Opera" in the West End and I didn't want to miss it.

The errant plane finally arrived, was cleaned with record speed, and we boarded slightly two hours behind schedule. If you are doing the math, this now left us with a very tight connection. I was sixty-one years old at the time. I know I set an Olympic record for a sixty-one-year-old women racing through George H.W. Bush Intercontinental airport to catch an international flight. But make it we did. Before we were wheels up, my husband was gently snoring in the seat beside me. Despite splurging on comfy seats in business class, I could not join in his sweet slumber. I tossed and turned for eight hours across the Atlantic and arrived at London Heathrow feeling like I had added twenty years on to my age count.

Everyone met up as scheduled, got to the hotel without incident and did some walking around and sightseeing to try to get on London time. We made a lengthy stop at Harrods, so I, the expectant grandmother, could pick up a few little things for my new granddaughter-to-be. Many, many English pounds later, I emerged from the world famous department store with enough stuffed animals to open a boutique, some indispensable outfits, and a sampling of British toys. I refrained reluctantly from the ever so lovely English pram (only because of packing restraints), and the Burberry romper, whose price would have paid for dinner that night.

Before we knew it, we were approaching dinnertime and our

show. I had been up for approximately thirty-eight hours at this point, run a marathon, flown over five thousand miles and shopped until I dropped. As a result, I slept through the last half of Phantom. That was a big mistake, because it was just enough to keep me awake for another thirty-eight hours.

The rest of the family decided to get up early that next day to visit a meat market and watch the butchering of the animals for restaurant menus. I stayed in bed, hoping to catch a nap after another sleepless night. I wanted to be at least semi-awake, for we had big plans for the evening.

My newlywed daughter had decided to surprise her foodie groom for his thirty-fifth birthday with an extravagant meal at Gordon Ramsay's famous restaurant at the Claridge's Hotel. She reserved the one table in the kitchen for a multi-course extravaganza, each course paired with wine. It was very expensive, so expensive in fact, she asked her dad ever so politely if he wouldn't mind picking up the wine tab. My husband was a sucker for any request from either of his daughters, and of course he said yes. So off we went. We were greeted in the lobby of the hotel by a lovely stiff upper-lipped gentleman, who guided us to banquette seating just outside the entrance to the restaurant. We were provided with amuse bouche (or in our language, appetizers). The sommelier instantly appeared and asked what we would like to order from their extensive wine menu to drink, showing my husband her selection, which I believe equated to about $200 a bottle. He politely demurred, citing a choice of his own. It should be noted that my husband was a wine connoisseur, and knew what he was talking about. He also knew when he was being upsold. At that moment, a battle of sorts engaged between the sommelier and the customer. Nothing she suggested would meet with his approval the rest of the night, and pretty much everything he asked for was met with an ever so slight roll of the eyes.

After our aperitifs and amuse bouches, we were led into the incredibly small kitchen with a secluded booth table tucked away in the corner. At that point the show really began, with course after course (and wine after wine) beautifully presented and consumed. Since our younger daughter was pregnant, she was unable to partake in any of the wine choices, and instead ordered non-alcoholic umbrella type drinks with each course, at the approximate cost of $20 per drink. Did I mention there were multiple courses? At one point, the gentlemen in our party were invited into the kitchen to help prepare a side dish of moshy peas, a British staple. Outfitted with obligatory aprons, their job was to finalize the presentation of the peas on the plate, deftly demonstrated by a sous chef utilizing two spoons. It was not as simple as it looked, and provided much hilarity. Just as they were admitting defeat, into the kitchen strolled comedian Adam Sandler, who we were later told had popped into the restaurant unannounced, requesting the kitchen table, only to be told it had already been booked for the evening. Apparently he wanted to come by and check out who had usurped his dinner table. When the first of three desserts was finally presented, along with the last of the bottles of dessert wine and the final umbrella drink, my husband was presented with the liquor bill. By this time the sommelier had softened, fully anticipating a hefty gratuity after eight, count them eight, bottles of purchased wine. As I saw the color completely drain from my husband's face, I knew we probably could have booked another vacation for what the wine cost. I wasn't far off!

After this memorable evening, it was time to head to the ship in

Southampton the next day. We resembled Mohammed crossing the Alps with our entourage of six adults, a menagerie of teddy bears and toys, two cars and drivers and an attached luggage cart. Embarkation went smoothly, and we were soon ensconced in our respective cabins and out exploring the ship. Such tranquility was not to last, however. After our first port of call in Guernsey in the Channel Islands, we all reconnoitered at a bar onboard ship for cocktails before dinner. My husband took issue with the noise volume of the canned music in said bar, and politely asked if it could be turned down. The bartender seemingly willingly obliged, and a few moments of softer music ensued. Five minutes later, it was at decibel level again. Again came a request to turn it down. This scenario repeated itself at least three times, with Jim egging my husband on, before my daughters and I grabbed all three of the boys and dragged them to the dining room - early.

It got even better after dinner. It was formal night, and we were all dressed to the nines. I had the brilliant idea to avail ourselves of the onboard photographer and get a formal portrait of our family. The gentlemen were not terribly onboard with this plan, but they humored me. When our turn came, the photographer started posing us: my husband seated in an overstuffed arm chair, me standing just to his left, the four adult children behind us. It was a pose reminiscent of the Carrington family from the "Dynasty" TV series. For some reason, however, she positioned the kids so they were not standing next to their spouses. Jim objected, pointing to his sister in law,

"But this isn't my wife. You put her over there by mistake."

The photographer didn't care; she liked her composition better than who was married to whom. The straw that broke the proverbial camel's back, however, was when she motioned to our older daughter, Jim's wife.

"You, the pretty, skinny one, please come more forward."

Remember I mentioned our younger daughter was pregnant? She was just beginning to show, felt fat, bloated, and unattractive (she wasn't). But that's the way she felt. She was wearing a black cocktail dress; her sister was wearing a long, white Grecian gown. She was hormonal and couldn't drink, and she was miserable. If I look closely, I swear I can see a tear in her eye in the photo. When the proofs came back, Kristy hated the picture. I thought the photo turned out great, and was a nice memory of our trip, so I ordered an oversize canvas that the cruise line would ship to us, at great cost, I might add. When it finally arrived, well over two months after we arrived home, it was of a totally different family! Many phone calls to the cruise line, and several months later, I finally received the correct canvas. My daughter still hates it.

The next day we were in Dublin, and everyone was looking forward to a pub-crawl that our son in law Martin had put together. But first we had to get off the ship. The ship's photographer - yes, the same one - had enlisted crew to dress up as leprechauns and greet the passengers as they disembarked the gangway. Passengers posed with the leprechauns and had their pictures taken. The idea of course was to sell these photos to the guests. Scott and I had gotten off a little early and were standing on the pier waiting for the kids. As we saw them emerge from the door, I starting taking a couple of photos. The photographer sprung from her perch and literally accosted me, telling me I was not allowed to take pictures. Mind you, I was not taking pictures of anybody posing with the leprechauns; I was simply taking pictures of my children emerging from the ship. My husband took issue, and a discussion ensued. It would have continued for some time, had the photographer and her leprechauns not realized that they were missing photo opportunities with the long stream of passengers still disembarking. We spent the rest of the day talking about Dad's fight with a leprechaun in Dublin. The story got more hilarious with every pub we hit.

We enjoyed many other ports on this trip, from Cobh and Belfast Ireland to Liverpool, England to Glasgow, Invergordon and Edinburgh, Scotland. We visited the Beatle's stomping ground and took obligatory photos at Strawberry Fields and Penny Lane. We learned about the still divided history of Northern Ireland, and climbed the Mile High Road to Edinburgh Castle. We tasted beer at the Guinness Distillery and Scotch at Glengoyne. Kristy drank water; umbrella drinks were not offered at either establishment. We searched for Nessie at Loch Ness sitting on the side pontoons of a high-speed inflatable boat, complete with insulated suits. I was positive my unborn granddaughter would be flung overboard and end up swimming in the cold waters with her mother and Nessie herself.

Finally, as the cruise was winding down, we were to dock at our last port of LeHavre, France. This was the jumping off stop for our visit to Normandy and the World War II beaches. For me, it was the highlight of the cruise and the main reason I had chosen the itinerary. Two nights before we were to dock, our captain decided that the weather was a bit too windy and he was canceling the port. Although I had sailed dozens of times, and I completely understood that the safety of the passengers is the top priority of any cruise line, I felt this was a ridiculous and unwarranted decision. We were in Edinburgh; LeHave was two days away. Yet, the captain decided to reroute us all the way BACK around the British Isles, from whence we had just come, to avoid some wind in the English Channel. Unfortunately, guests do not get to override the captain's decision. So back around Great Britain we went. The upside of this was it gave us two more sea days to eat, drink and be merry. The downside, besides missing the port for which I had booked the cruise, was that there were two more days to eat, drink and be merry. And pay for the drinks. We celebrated Jim's actual birthday one of those nights in the Italian specialty restaurant, and I'm pretty sure caused everybody else to leave early due to our frivolity. We finally ended up back in Southampton and made a quick visit to Windsor Castle before our return to London and our flights back home. It was a memorable trip: Martin was dubbed our map-reader; Kristy and her baby were our bathroom finders; Ginger was our in house photographer, and Jim was our eater. Scott was our wine guy and instigator. And me? Well, I got to enjoy it all.

26 LEARNING JOURNEY/KITCHEN REMODEL

*Living through a home renovation is like living in the wild...you do whatever it takes to
survive.*

Author unknown

W hen in the course of human events it becomes necessary to take the painful plunge and do something about the outdated, nonfunctional space that is your kitchen, it can be a simple or not so simple affair. Step one was convincing my husband this was a necessary upgrade. Having done some minor changes not too many years previous, he remained unconvinced until I suggested that the icky closet that was being used for a pantry be demolished to make room for a large standup wine refrigerator. Voila! Husband was on board. Next, not wanting to spend a large fortune on a house that was approaching its third decade, but needing (wanting) more space for my many dishes, my husband's myriad of electrical appliances and gadgets, and generally a better traffic flow and organization, we decided to undertake what we thought would be a simple cosmetic overhaul. We didn't want to do anything drastic like move walls and such; we just wanted new cabinets, countertops and backsplash. We even planned on keeping most of our appliances, and our existing floor. How hard could this possibly be? Well, there was the minor detail of also wanting to remove the 1980's soffits and pot shelves, but that was nothing a little sledgehammer couldn't solve.

We began the process with a budget in mind and a visit to a local custom furniture store. Said store had built us an entertainment unit several years prior, which we loved. We thought they would be a good choice so that we could match the new cabinets to the entertainment unit. We were in no particular hurry (this first trip was in October, 2010, and we were hoping to start actual work at the end of January, 2011). Our helpful saleslady subsequently visited our home, designed new cabinets, suggested moving our refrigerator, and gave me pretty drawings, which I stared at for hours at a time, deciding which set of dishes would go where. We made some adjustments, added a spice drawer and a sink tip-out among other things, and she gave us a price. We were thrilled to discover we were within our budget. Feeling warm and fuzzy about the whole project, we signed a contract by the end of December. We were told to expect four to five weeks from demolition to completion. It sounded quite reasonable at the time.

The first step was a field measure, followed by a meeting at the factory to go over all the specs. Here's where we ran into the first hiccup. We learned among other things that sink installation is different from sink hookup (who knew?), that under cabinet lighting which we thought was included, wasn't), that the sink tip-out was now extra. After some negotiation, we left the meeting with a little more than $1000 added to our invoice.

Demolition began pretty much on schedule and was not as bad as expected. It was noisy and dirty, but over with quickly. This, however, was followed by two days of fiesta style music while workers repaired drywall, textured and repainted the walls. Two days from seven am to seven pm, I might add. While my husband beat a hasty retreat to his downtown office, my only respite was the approximate two-hour lunchtime siesta in my driveway.

Because we were moving our refrigerator from one wall to another, it was necessary to add some tile where cabinets were removed. The tile on our floor was put in by an Armenian craftsman several years previous, and was on special because it was being discontinued. We had several pieces left, more than enough to fix this area of the floor. However, as our handyman was working, he discovered that the floor was uneven, and the aforesaid Armenian craftsman had glued two tiles together in several places to even things up. Each time our handyman chipped at a tile, another one cracked. He determined he needed to rent a jackhammer to get the stuff up, and hoped that the tiles would stop cracking at some point. I hoped so too, since three-quarters of the square footage of our home was covered in this tile, and I knew I didn't have enough to redo the entire house. I saw our budget blowing up and new floors having to be laid throughout. I called my husband in a panic, and he came home from downtown to try to solve the problem. It was not my finest hour. As it turned out, the double gluing only extended a few square feet, and the floor crisis ended as quickly as it began. It was still not my finest hour.

While the kitchen was being ripped apart, my makeshift kitchen consisted of two pantry areas: one on a card table in the garage, and the other on the patio table. The laundry room sink became the place to wash any dishes. We stocked up on paper plates and cups. On those rare occasions when I just had to use a real plate we utilized the most basic garbage disposal/dishwashing combination of all: our two dogs, who were thrilled with their new duties.

The next step was cabinet installation. Specs for all appliances had been submitted and the custom cabinets were field measured and checked and rechecked. They didn't fit, at least four of them didn't. One was too big, two were two small and one was too tall. My husband made another trip back home from downtown and met with supervisors who came out to work the problem.

Back to the factory they went. While they are all getting trimmed or stretched or trashed or whatever is done to rejected cabinets, the granite installation date now had to be rescheduled since one can't install granite when there are no cabinets to put it on.

I must digress here for a moment to actually discuss the granite selection. It was not a fun process. I selected the tile backsplash first, and then matched the granite to it. However, the backsplash turned out to be unavailable, so we needed to start from scratch. Running up against a deadline, I utilized the services of a designer, got quotes for three or four different granite selections and finally narrowed it down to one. All along I was given prices for two slabs of granite, with an option for a possible third. We also were given a quote to purchase and install our mere twenty-eight square feet of backsplash, all through the furniture company. When it came time to template the granite, the quote now changed from two slabs, pick a third, to one slab, pay for the second. Oh, and by the way, we were informed, the backsplash quote increased by $2500 for a cheaper tile than I had originally chosen. Furious, my husband worked his way through employees at the factory until he got to the general manager, who met with the saleslady, who met with the foreman, who met with the field measurer, who met with the kitchen supervisor, who met with Pluto for all we knew. End result: they knocked a few things off the invoice, we caved on the granite prices and purchased our own tile, which we ended up having installed privately for a fraction of their price. More important end result: VERY bad taste in our mouth over the practices of the furniture company. No more warm and fuzzies.

Cabinets were now remade and installed, granite was templated, the floor repaired. Electricians and plumbers were in and out, after a no-show, a re-do and a bad fitting. It was finally time to install the appliances. The first thing that happened was that the microwave oven panel broke while installing the vent. Then the new fridge arrived. The cabinetry surrounding it was supposed to do just that, surround it. Only it didn't. We easily had four to five inches of lovely gray refrigerator siding showing. Another phone call to the furniture company. "Hmmm", they said. Back out came the field measurer, who determined this cabinet too must be uninstalled and a new one put in its place. Sigh.

It was about this time that we received an email stating that the granite fabricator was running behind and our granite would now be delayed by about a week. Perfect. We moved heaven and earth and my husband had taken yet more time off work to go to the fabricator's to lay out the template to meet their schedule. But now THEY were running behind. This was another one of my not so fine moments. I still had no working dishwasher, or sink, and it was now late March. We were nine weeks into the four to five that were promised. Once the granite was finally installed, the plumbers and electricians came back to get me some running water, and the handyman returned to put in the backsplash and tile mural. My husband happily started moving his wine into its new home. It was all worth it, right hon? We immediately got another email from our not-so-favorite furniture company, indicating that they would like to come out the next day to receive their final payment. We made them wait a week. It seemed only fair; after all, I think they took YEARS off my life!

My dishwashers

27 SECOND CHANCE JOURNEY/WHEN THE CASSEROLES STOP COMING

Accept what is, let go of what was, and have faith in what will be.

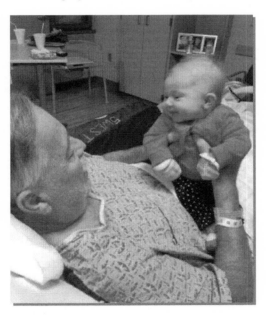

Scott recuperating in the hospital with our new granddaughter, 2013

F

ebruary 14, 2013 began just like every other weekday. It was a Thursday, and we were leaving the next day for a much-anticipated long weekend in Napa. My husband was up a little later than usual, but he wished me a Happy Valentine's Day, got in the shower and started getting ready for work. What happened next changed our lives forever.

The crash sounded like a tray of glass breaking. I yelled,

"What did you drop?"

No answer. As I peered over the bed into the dressing area I saw his crumbled form on the ceramic tile floor, blood oozing onto the shirts waiting to be taken to the cleaners. The ambulance came in minutes. Minutes after that we were in the ER. Family members arrived seconds after that. Calls went out to those who needed to know. It was a whirlwind of activity. And it was standing around doing nothing. It was scores of doctors and other medical personnel. It was machines and tubes and foreign smells. It was a fear I had never felt before.

Several hours later we had our diagnosis: the fall had caused a traumatic brain injury. He had bleeding in his brain and was having seizures. The fall itself was caused by acute anemia, and a large bleeding ulcer had caused the anemia. And just for fun, let's add extreme hypertension into the mix. In short, he was a mess. To put him back together again required a twelve day stay in ICU, followed by two weeks as an inpatient in an acute rehab facility, followed by one week at home, then another week in the hospital for a blood clot in the leg. He was off work for six weeks, and struggled for months with a weak neck, poor range of motion and double vision. Follow up doctors' visits and therapy continued and were our norm for well over two years.

This all happened because my husband was a man who avoided doctors at all costs. He ignored his ulcer symptoms until he could ignore them no longer. Then he self-treated them with Excedrin until he passed out. For someone who didn't like doctors, he sure got to know a lot of them intimately after that fateful day.

While he was being well taken care of in the hospital, I was being well taken care of by family and friends. My daughters arranged a food chain of sorts, and chicken casseroles and lasagnas kept appearing until my freezer, and my heart, were overflowing. There were other wonderful food gift items as well, things like potato cheese soup and banana bread and popcorn tins, all of which warmed our hearts as well as our ribs. I don't know what I would have done without them and the people that sent them. My mom and my sister called daily, sometimes more than once, and offered a sounding board for my frustration and fears. Dear friends came to the hospital just to sit with me or grab a bite in the cafeteria. My niece, a nurse at Mayo, stopped by ICU as often as she could, helping me understand the maze of medical terms and procedures. Emails and texts from all over the country never failed to cheer me up. Our daughters and sons-in-law were by my side throughout each hospital stay, day and night. Just as my husband would not have survived had it not been for his team of health care professionals, I would not have survived were it not for our kids, our family and our friends. I owe them a debt of gratitude I can never repay.

With my husband's health crisis came many lessons. I was reminded that life is indeed fragile, that it can change on the turn of a dime, and that it is to be celebrated and cherished. I learned that when you need it the most, God might just send you an angel. Mine came in the form of our lead doctor at Mayo. First of all, he spoke to me in English, not medical-ese. He comforted me, eased my fears, and was eternally optimistic, yet straightforward. He told me that he thought by mid-summer this would all be a bad memory. I needed to hear that during those dark days. He also kept in touch with us after my husband was released, which is unheard of for most doctors. He gave me his private cell phone number and home email address. He wrote a back to work release letter for us. In short, he cared. I will never forget him, for he got me through the roughest times.

As we approached the end of May that year, three months into our new normal, the get-well cards, the chicken casseroles and the lasagnas had long since stopped coming. So now what? Our new life was not one that we had planned, asked for or anticipated. We gave up a lot: our Diamondbacks' season tickets that year, a trip we had planned to Europe, the lifestyle we had gotten used to and enjoyed, just as a few examples. But those were just things. We were facing catastrophic medical bills and "discussions" with the insurance company over who was going to pay them; we now scheduled our lives around doctors' appointments, therapy appointments and pharmacy pickups. Despite all that, we were lucky. He was alive. His brain was working. We had every reason to expect a full recovery. In a way, his accident was even a blessing. Forced from the law firm where he was a shareholder (editorial comment: who does that?), but was not really happy, he found a new job that was close to home. And, while no one anticipates starting again at his age, it was a good fit for him. He once again enjoyed going to work in the morning, which eased his stress, which helped his healing. He knew he was fortunate, and he no longer fought going to a doctor. He had no choice, but he did it without complaining. We cherished the time spent with our kids and grandkids even more than before if that was possible. And we took it one day at a time. That's a cliché, I know, but it's what worked for us. Some days were better than others, for both of us. But we picked our way through all the rubble left by our own personal tornado, and tried to rebuild, one step at a time. Yes, we were lucky indeed. We were given the gift of four more years, and I was taught lessons that would serve me well later when I needed them most.

28 LIFE JOURNEY/'TIL DEATH DO US PART

The trouble is, you think you have time.

Buddha

Our last photo together, Nashville, March 2017

I n the four years after my husband's catastrophic accident, we tried to live life again, although there were continual challenges. After numerous hospital stays, and both inpatient and outpatient therapy, he had recovered enough that he was able to return to work and begin normal activity.

Although to the outside world Scott appeared to be his old self, those of us closest to him noticed small differences. His sense of humor, while not gone, was greatly diminished. He could not tolerate a lot of noise. He slept more than usual. At times, he would stare off into the distance, then snap back and join us again. The law firm where he had been a shareholder for ten years forced him out, without ceremony, and he had to find another job. It was humiliating for him.

But we moved on. Grateful for this second chance at life, we paid off debt that had accumulated, saved the social security income that we both started taking a few months later, enjoyed our grandkids, and traveled as often as we could. He took his medication, kept his follow up doctor appointments and generally felt well. We had four more pretty good years.

The first sign that something was not right was during a trip to Nashville in March 2017. We were there to oversee the recording of an album for our friend and cruise director Eric De Gray, who we had met several years before. We believed in his talent, and offered to match him up with our producer friend, Ron Fairchild, who was also the longtime piano player for the Oak Ridge Boys. We all met up in Nashville, and laid down tracks for the CD in four days. Our last day in town was a sightseeing day, and as Eric and I walked slightly ahead, Scott stumbled down a couple of stairs and fell. He wasn't hurt and claimed he was fine; that he had just worn the wrong shoes. Later, Eric told me that he had noticed Scott staring off, unseeing, a few times at dinner that week.

When we got home, I noticed within a few days that Scott's right leg appeared swollen. This was the same leg where he had suffered a blood clot four years previous. My suggestions to get it checked out were met with stubborn resistance. "I'm fine", he insisted. It didn't feel warm to the touch like the last time, so I let it go.

The evening of April 16, 2017, we enjoyed a quiet dinner on our patio; talked to Eric on the phone about the masters of the CD we had just received, and watched some television. Scott fell asleep on the couch (a regular habit) and just before midnight, woke up and said he was going to bed.

I replied, "I'm going to take the dog out and I will be right behind you."

Not more than three minutes later, I made my way to the bedroom and heard Scott snoring, but it was not his usual sound.

"How in the world could he have fallen asleep this fast?" I thought.

I shook him a little, but there was no response. I shook harder. Nothing. I yelled at him to wake up, and shook as hard as I could. There still was no response other than the weird "snoring" noise, but that was getting softer. Realizing something was very wrong, I grabbed my phone and called 911.

The next five hours were a total blur. Paramedics arrived quickly and worked on him until they could get a pulse. The ambulance rushed both of us to the hospital where we were met by one of my daughters and her husband. Doctors worked on him, both in emergency and ICU for hours and at one point I remember someone telling me he had been without oxygen to the brain for over thirty minutes. While I knew the ramifications of that, it didn't register. At 5:30 A.M., I gave the okay to remove him from life support, and he died within a few minutes, just before my older daughter got to the hospital.

His life was over at the age of 68. The subsequent autopsy report showed that death was a result of arteriosclerosis and a pulmonary embolism, aggravated by chronic seizures, most likely as a result of the previous brain injury. My life, and my children and grandchildren's lives were changed forever. We had been married just two months shy of forty-five years. We all had plans.

29 DEATH JOURNEY/PLANNING A FUNERAL

A funeral is not a day in a lifetime; it is a lifetime in a day.

The first thing a surviving family member has to do when a loved one dies is plan the funeral. Most of us are in no condition to do this at that particular time, and if the deceased hasn't expressed his or her preferences, it makes the task all the more difficult.

After the recovery from Scott's initial accident four years earlier, we were lulled into a sense of security, never dreaming that he wouldn't live at least another decade or perhaps more. We were enjoying the extra years we had been given. Plus, he would never entertain discussing the dreaded topic of "arrangements." Occasionally when I heard a song I'd like, an artist I was fond of, or a quote that moved me, I'd say,

"I'd like to have that played/sung/recited at my funeral. How about you?"

"Uh huh" was usually the best response I could hope for, and then silence or change of subject.

When he died suddenly at the age of 68, I was at a loss and totally unprepared for the days ahead. One night he was here, and the next night he wasn't. A day later I found myself at a funeral home planning his memorial service with absolutely no earthly idea what he would have wanted. My daughters and I sat across from a very serious man who pushed a box of tissues in our direction, although all three of us were dry-eyed at the time. There were forms to fill out, with statistics such as social security number, birth date, parents' names, and then the gut puncher: date of death. The man I had been married to for almost forty-five years had been summarized on one 8x11 sheet of paper.

Next came the questions. Do you want the service here? A church? Burial or cremation? Casket or urn? Do you have a clergyman? Can you bring in some pictures? What about a video tribute? Obituary in the paper? Flowers? Would you like to see our Butterfly Garden?

"I don't know, I don't know, I don't know and sure let's go look at the Butterfly Garden." I silently screamed.

An hour or so later we had made our decisions. The only thing I knew for sure was that my husband wanted to be cremated. Everything else we sort of guessed at, and to be honest, many of those decisions were financially based. The Butterfly Garden was actually quite serene, so that became his final resting place, save for a few vials of ashes I requested for scattering later. We opted for a memorial service in a church several days later. I chose the music; my kids planned the reception. I put together a slide show and we had a tribute from the grandkids, a couple of readings and some eulogies. I don't know if he would have chosen any of these things.

I've heard it said that the funeral or memorial service is really for the living, not the dead. But it is a burden on the living to play twenty questions when you don't really know the answers, and because of the nature of the game, you will never know if you actually got them right.

I also learned that no matter how sympathetic people may seem, everyone has their hand out. In my experience, the funeral home itemized charges for everything, as did the church. From cremation costs to the box that was required, to the use of their facilities, to the urn or casket to the burial plot, to the death certificates, nothing was "included." Well, maybe the box of tissues, but probably even that charge was hidden in there somewhere. The church charged for the use of their space, the audiovisual people, and the clergy even though we brought our own officiant. They offered musicians (at a cost of course), but I opted for recorded music that a Nashville friend made for me. Then there were the flowers, the programs, the guest book, the reception cards, and the list went on. If there is a reception afterward, there is the cost of the venue, food and beverage and cleanup. We had my husband's reception at my daughter's home, but still needed to provide food and drink, and opted to employ a caterer and bartender. Funerals are not cheap, even if you try to be economical. My husband had made no provision for this; luckily I had a savings account I could tap into for the almost $10,000 in costs.

Here are a few things you can do (write them down) to make it easier on your survivors:

1. Choose how your remains will be handled, burial or cremation. (At least I knew this much)

2. Decide if you want a service and if so, what kind. You don't need to plan the whole thing from beginning to end, just outline the basics.

3. Pick a song or two that you like.

4. Pick a verse or two that you like.

5. If there is anything special you want done or said, or not done or said, make note of it.

6. Finally and quite important, put a little money aside or in a cookie jar somewhere for this wonderful tribute to your life. Funerals are expensive!

30 LEARNING JOURNEY/IS YOUR FINANCIAL HOUSE IN ORDER?

Not everything that counts can be counted, and not everything that can be counted counts.

Albert Einstein

M aking sure your financial house is in order before your die (and let's face it, none of us are going to be exempt from this journey) is a great gift you can leave to your surviving loved ones, particularly is you are the primary earner. And being proactive as the potential survivor is a responsibility and gift you can give yourself. I can speak to this because neither of those things was true in my situation.

My husband had a lot of wonderful qualities: he was gregarious, kind, funny, generous and protective of his family. He was a great lawyer, and very few people who knew him disliked him. But as I was soon to find out, financial acuity was not one of his skills. It isn't necessary to detail all the surprises that came my way within a short time of his death, and I will not do so for the sake of my children and grandchildren. They adored their father and grandfather, and he was without doubt one of the best examples of both those titles. Nothing that he did or didn't do can take that away, and I will not do so here.

Suffice it to say that when he died, my income stopped, and stopped cold. Although we were both drawing social security, the rules state that if one spouse dies, the surviving spouse retains the higher of the two checks, but cannot keep both. Therefore, I kept his and lost mine, a reduction of about one-third of what we were receiving every month. In addition, there was less life insurance than I thought, bills I did not know about, the cost of the funeral, and income taxes that needed to be paid. At the same time, the mortgage statements, the monthly bills and the daily living expenses kept coming relentlessly. Creditors do not care if the primary breadwinner has died.

I learned a lot, and I learned it quickly. The lessons were painful, life-changing and on-going. Here are a few of the suggestions I can give from my experience:

Wills and Directives

Don't procrastinate. Just get them done, keep them in a safe place and tell your loved ones where to find them. I am still looking for the originals of ours, years later.

Usernames and Passwords

No matter if you use your dog's name or a complicated series of codes and numbers, store all necessary usernames and passwords in a safe place and let your loved ones know where to find them. Make sure they know how to get into your computer, laptop and/or tablet or phone. Reducing your survivors to playing a guessing game is frustrating at best. There are apps to make this easy.

Bank accounts and Safe Deposit Boxes

Make sure these are either in joint tenancy with your partner, or he/she is an authorized user, although even the latter is by far foolproof. At one bank my husband had an account in his name only. I brought in a death certificate and they cut a check to me for the balance on the spot and provided me with copies of statements for the previous year for tax purposes. It took about ten minutes. Another bank, where he had three accounts, but I was only a joint owner on one (even though all were linked and I had access to all of them for years), insisted on a letter from a lawyer stating that he was the sole owner of his business account. Holding the death certificate in his hands, the bank officer told me with a straight face that the only way he could release the funds to me was if he talked to the account holder himself. When I incredulously explained that might be a bit difficult since he was dead, and you are holding his bleeping death certificate in your bleeping hand, I was told that was state law and bank policy. It took four hours, two trips, that letter from the attorney, an affidavit and not a few tears to get them to release the funds. So apparently it wasn't state policy or bank policy after all, because as far as I know they were never able to contact my deceased husband.

In going through papers I found an invoice dated four years previous for a safe deposit box. Knowing nothing about it, I called the bank only to discover they could not locate an existing account with that box number. So was it closed, or are there important documents somewhere? I don't know, and I'm not sure I ever will.

Life Insurance and other safeguards

Unless you are blessed with a generous pension, make sure you have life insurance, annuities, profit sharing, 401k's or something for your survivor to fall back on if your paychecks suddenly cease. Period. And have more than you think you need. If you are the primary breadwinner, the sudden loss of your income will provide an incredible hardship on your survivors without this cushion. Remember that the mortgage, utilities, service people, taxes, home insurance, car payments and everything else will keep coming like clockwork, month after month. These creditors will not give one hoot that you have died and your paycheck has stopped. My household income went from six figures to a reduced social security check overnight. Protecting those you love is a responsibility you should not shirk.

Credit card debt

Be current and timely with your payments. Pay your charges off in their entirety every month if you possibly can. Those credit card bills are going to keep coming as well after you die. If they are in your name only, your spouse may not be responsible. But joint accounts and authorized user accounts will be the responsibility of the survivor. And there are nine states (Arizona, California, Idaho, Louisiana, Nevada, New Mexico, Texas, Washington and Wisconsin) where community property laws state that your spouse IS responsible for your solo debts. Don't do that to someone you love.

Taxes

There are two truisms of life, as we all know: death and taxes. Pay them, and be current. If your employer is not already taking deductions for you with each paycheck, make sure you set aside money for the federal deductions. Depending on your tax bracket, that obligation can add up quickly, and cause real sticker shock when it is time to pay Uncle Sam. And one way or another, someone is always going to have to pay Uncle Sam. Leave copies of past years taxes where they can easily be found. Make sure all receipts; deductions, W2's, 1099's and the like are in an easily found location as well. There is nothing worse than either scrambling at the last minute to gather all that information or a surprise tax liability in the tens of thousands of dollars.

Surviving Spouse Responsibility

The preceding is what you can do as the person who is going to die. The surviving spouse, however, has responsibilities as well, and I accept full responsibility for not doing some of these things.

1. Ask what those passwords are, and make sure you have access to them. You will need them to get into bank accounts, utility accounts, mortgage accounts, credit card accounts, doctor portals, social security, and cable TV accounts. If your spouse died tomorrow, could you readily access all of these?

2. As the survivor, you should know about all household and business bank accounts. Have a frank discussion with your spouse and make sure you are knowledgeable about this. Find out what life insurance you have and discuss as a couple whether it is wise or cost effective to have more. Keep a copy of the policies in the home so you have ready access, and know where the originals are.

3. Know what your credit card debt obligations are. The best way to do this is pull your respective credit reports regularly. This is also good practice to determine if anything is being reported erroneously.

4. Make sure you see a copy of your income taxes when they are due in April (or October if you have filed an extension). Know where the receipts for the year are and double check that they have been organized properly for easy access.

5.   Understand social security benefits and the restrictions. Be aware that the death benefit for the surviving spouse is only $255. If you are both collecting social security, you will receive the higher of the two checks, but not both. Since we were both collecting at the time of my husband's death, I was awarded his amount, but mine was discontinued, resulting in a net loss of income to me. Also be aware that social security is taxable up to eighty-five per cent, depending on your tax bracket. That's another kick in the teeth. Be prepared for it.

6. Finally, if you are a partner in a relationship and will bear any kind of financial responsibility upon that person's death, find a good financial advisor, no matter what your assets may be. Their advice can be invaluable. And live by the words of President Ronald Reagan; "trust, but verify." Always verify. It could make the difference between financial security in your golden years - or not.

31 GRIEF JOURNEY/HOW TO HELP A GRIEVING FRIEND

Maybe I can't stop the downpour, but I will always walk with you in the rain.

So many of my loved ones asked me in the aftermath of my husband's death, "What can I do?"

This open letter to my family and friends was an attempt to answer that well-meaning question. Its tenets are as true long after the death of a loved one as they are in the first gut-

196

wrenching days and weeks, for there is no timetable for mourning. Months, and years after the death, you still wake up alone; you still prepare meals for one and fight loneliness with each one of them. You still struggle with the realities of life without your spouse, you still have no one to take out the trash or fix a toilet or service the car, or whatever else were the "normal" jobs your spouse performed. Going out to dinner or a movie or traveling has changed, and it's lonelier. Friends and family are well meaning and usually sympathetic to the newly bereaved needs, but often just don't know how to act on those feelings. I hope this letter provides some insight:

My Dear Family and Friends:

Please understand that my world as I knew it is in shambles. I no longer feel secure. My home no longer feels like my home. Every bit of my daily life has changed. Dinnertime is quiet and lonely, because nobody walks through the door at the end of the day. Big things and little things alike overwhelm me. I'm sorry for my tears, but I cannot control them. They often appear when least expected. I'm (insert number of months/years) into this now and grief still comes at me in waves and when it hits, it hits hard. I never know when a wave is coming and I just have to ride it out until the sea is calm again. When the tears come, I will love you for simply allowing me to shed them. There is nothing you need to say.

Just please don't abandon me. Feeling alone and that no one understands is debilitating. No one can really understand of course unless they are in my shoes, and I wouldn't wish that on any one of you. My world is painful. Don't be afraid of me. I don't have a disease. If you don't know what to say, that's ok. A simple hug means the world. Physical contact is healing. Even "I'm sorry" or "I don't know what to say" speaks volumes. Thank you for all the shoulders that have been offered.

Just because my hair is done and I have makeup on does not mean that I am ok. Only ask me how I'm doing if you really want to know. I appreciate it when you say, "You're so strong." I know you are trying to boost my spirits. But I do not feel strong. I am overwhelmed by almost everything in my life right now. Sometimes I am numb and simply cannot function, which drives me nuts. All my life I've prided myself in making lists of lists, and systematically checking the items off with a feeling of accomplishment. (I have always been a little OCD). Now small tasks take up all my energy. Some days I cannot eat because food is tasteless or sits like a rock in my stomach; other days I binge on unhealthy snacks because I don't have the energy to prepare a meal for one. There are nights when my mind races and memories haunt me and worries consume me so that I cannot sleep. There are other days I have to force myself to get out of bed.

I don't know when or if or how I will heal from this. Please be patient with me, even though I know that is asking a lot. I know you all have your lives to live and your trials as well. I understand the world does not revolve around me, nor do I want it to. I am just searching for a new way to belong.

I am not only grieving a death, but life as I knew it as well. I am grieving the life we built together, the plans that we had, the places we were going to go, the experiences we were going to share. I loved our life. Now I have to build a new one for myself, alone. The very thought of that panics me every day.

Yes, I am trying to "get on with my life." I am doing that every second of every day. I am doing things I never thought I would have to do, and nothing is easy. NOTHING is easy.

Despite all that, my heart is full with the kindnesses so many of you have shown me. I am beyond blessed that my family lives close by and have taken over so many chores, both mundane and difficult, with which I have been completely unable to cope.

I am so lucky to be able to spend quality time with five beautiful grandchildren, who never fail to bring a smile to my face even on the darkest of days.

I give thanks every day for those friends I know I can call any time day or night, who will listen to my sorrows, offer a shoulder for my tears, and bring a smile to my face. I am also grateful to so many others for time they have given, advice they have shared, and love they have showered on me.

I am lucky to have several of my husband's colleagues who have facilitated things I could never hope to understand, ranging from finances to real estate to termites.

But please know that if you say "Call me if you need anything, I probably won't. First of all, I rarely have any idea what I need. If you think of something, just do it. One friend bought theater tickets, and gave me the date and the time she was going to pick me up. All I had to do was get dressed and enjoy an evening with her. Another, in the midst of her own house move, dropped everything and went on a trip with me so I would not be alone so soon after my husband's death. Gestures don't have to be that grandiose. Anything, so long as it shows you are thinking of me, is so appreciated. If you feel like calling me, please do; you won't be bothering me. I love phone calls when I am least expecting them from old friends. They brighten my day, or make my evening a little less lonely. I look forward to the emails and texts and messages I get from special friends almost every day. Hearing about what is going on in your lives allows me to feel in touch and helps me focus on something other than my own problems. Ask me more than once if I want to go to a movie or lunch or dinner or happy hour. I may say no at first, but please keep asking. It might just be a bad day for me. Someday I will say yes; just don't give up on me. I need to feel your hugs and your presence. I need you just to be with me. I need to know that you care about me.

So thank you all, and please, just love me the way I am today if you can, and know that with your love and support, joy will slowly return to my life.

My love to all of you,

Holly

32 DOWNSIZING JOURNEY/TOO MUCH STUFF

Sometimes the best way to grow is to subtract.

New beginnings

O ne of the painful truths facing me after the death of my husband was that I was going to have to move. First of all, the house was just too big for one person. Secondly, I could no longer afford it. Everything I had heard and read about the death of a spouse indicated that major decisions like these should be put off for a year. Unfortunately, I did not have that luxury. Therefore, two months after I became a widow, and on the day that would have been my forty-fifth anniversary, an auction was held in my home, divesting me of about sixty per cent of my worldly goods. I was reminded of the George Carlin classic comedy routine called "Stuff." One of the best lines, because it is so true, is "your house is nothing more than a pile of stuff with a cover on it."

The auction process itself was a nightmare. A swarm of people descended on my home and sorted through everything I owned, placing like items in "lots." One of the reasons I chose the auction method over an estate sale was that the company promised that 98% of the items would sell. I did not think to ask in my altered state exactly how they were going to accomplish this feat. I was just happy to know I wouldn't have to figure out how to pack, give away, sell or otherwise dispose of it all.

On the day of the auction, I was able to watch the bidding process online. One of the first "lots" to be sold was my husband's suits. He had been an attorney, and dressed the part. He didn't own designer clothes, but he did have nice ones. Imagine my dismay when his suits sold for $1.00, not per suit, but $1.00 for the entire lot! It soon went from the unbelievable to the ridiculous, and I powered down the computer. In short, I got rid of clothes, small appliances, wedding gifts, paintings, knick-knacks, a record collection, dishes, luggage, and rooms full of furniture, and made less money for all of it than it cost me to paint a few rooms in my house to get it ready to put on the market.

Thank goodness for my sister that day, her pool and copious

amounts of wine. Suffice it to say I thought I had sufficiently "downsized" my stuff and that I would be prepared for the move to a smaller space.

I thought wrong. The first clue was right in front of my eyes in my "packing notebook." Organization is one of my attributes; some would say obsession. Each box was labeled by number and room with the contents meticulously listed in the notebook, box by box. All one hundred thirty-seven of them. Yes, I was moving to a 1500 square foot house with one hundred thirty-seven boxes! That's a lot of stuff.

Four bedrooms had become three, three baths had become two, a family room and dining room were now one room. Undaunted however, I plunged head first into the unpacking process. At first it was fun to unwrap each piece of glassware, each treasure, each memory and find a new home for it. At first. Very quickly the shelves filled up with glasses and dishes and coffee mugs and "stuff." I scratched my head as I unwrapped over a dozen coffee mugs. Most were mismatched, but represented a memory of some kind. One mug was from the 2008 inauguration of President Bush, another from a trip to New Orleans, a couple represented our friends the Oak Ridge Boys, four were from the Diamondbacks as perks to season ticket holders, two more from Toronto, gifts from a friend. But there is just one of me. Did I actually need a dozen coffee mugs? I probably had disposed of twice that many at the auction. But they all meant something to me. So they made the move. And so it went, with everything.

Dishes, for example. There were the everyday ones, and then another full set with a French chef motif. And the hand painted ones from Italy, a souvenir from a favorite trip. There was my grandmother's priceless Limoges china, my wedding china, and the Spode Christmas dishes. Ack! Too much stuff. But I loved them all.

Then there were the linens. I probably sold twenty tablecloths with matching napkins. Yet I must have at least fifteen left, along with matching placemats. My house is too small to use the table leaves for the dining room table, thus rendering half of the linens I kept useless. Double ack!

And so it went. Box by box, shelf by crowded shelf, closet by stuffed closet. After everything was unpacked, I was thanking God for the storage cabinets in the garage. They now held all the stuff that wouldn't fit in the house. I had too much stuff! The irony however, is that incomprehensibly I needed more stuff. Really. I needed to buy a TV, a kitchen table, a breakfast nook, rugs for the family room, a medicine cabinet for the guest bath. You know why? I sold all that "stuff" at the auction!

33 DAUGHTER JOURNEY/MISSING MOM

Her absence is like the sky, spread over everything.

C.S. Lewis

With my Mom, 1949

M y mother passed away in 2014 after a nine-month battle with lung cancer that had metastasized to her hip. We only discovered it when she experienced excruciating pain in her hip shortly after Thanksgiving the year before that just would not go away. Test after test and treatment after treatment discovered nothing and did nothing for her pain. Finally, just after Christmas, she broke her hip and was scheduled for surgery right after the holidays. During that surgery, the cancer was discovered, and subsequent tests finally determined that the primary site was in fact her lung.

She had been a smoker much of her adult life, but had quit decades previously. Every winter for years though, she would develop a nagging cough. Repeated attempts to get her to check it out were met with resistance, or a shrug, and the standard comment, "I was just at the doctor, and he said everything is fine." I believe she knew deep down what the cough meant, but chose to ignore it and live her life unimpeded by doctors and treatments and surgeries and medications as long as she could. And she did just that.

After the hip surgery and subsequent stint at an inpatient rehab hospital (which she hated), she had some pretty good months. My sister and I made the difficult decision that she could no longer live alone in her home, and since her diagnosis was terminal, moved her into a wonderful, caring assisted living facility. She resisted that move with everything she had. The most independent, feisty woman I knew had gone from living in her own home to surgery, a terminal diagnosis and an uprooting move in less than two month's time. I would have been cranky too. But she also was suffering from dementia, which was getting worse by the week, and she was ninety years old. Difficult as it was, the move was for the best.

I don't think she ever got to the point where she liked her new surroundings, but she did adjust to them and make some new friends. She never participated in any of the group activities, preferring to stay in her room and read, but she was able to vociferously object when she discovered that dinner service was from four pm to seven pm every day. Our mother never, ever ate dinner before seven pm; it was simply uncivilized. There had to be time for cocktails first of course. So, this stubborn woman would many times have her cocktail while watching the news, then saunter downstairs to the dining room at precisely seven o'clock, the last possible moment. In a short time, the staff knew that they would be having one last diner before close; everyone knew to wait for Marian to make her appearance.

Eventually, the cancer took its toll, the dementia worsened, and hospice was brought in. After celebrating her ninety-first birthday with family on two consecutive nights at the same restaurant, she passed away a few weeks later. That last celebration was a study in contrasts. My sister and I thought combining both of our families with all Mom's great-grandchildren, who numbered seven at the time, all under the age of seven, would be too much for her in her frail state. Since she loved seafood, we each decided to take her out to dinner on subsequent nights, one family at a time. My husband and I went for the low-key approach and invited our kids and grandkids over to the house for cocktails and presents, and then took Mom to Red Lobster for a quiet dinner with just the three of us. She seemed to have a wonderful time, consuming one and a half orders of crab legs, along with a couple of hefty pours of Chardonnay. The next night my sister continued the celebration, also at Red Lobster, not knowing we had just been there the night before. I think Mom was worn out from our dinner; that night with my sister's family, she was listless, and ate little. She died less than three weeks later.

I didn't cry when my mother died; I guess I did most of my mourning during the months she was sick. But oh, how I miss her now. How I would like to have her here to discuss all the things that have happened in the last couple of years. What would she think of my challenges? Would she be sympathetic? Would she be angry with my husband? Would she tell me to stop whining and get my act together? I'm guessing the answer would be "yes" to all of those questions.

When I was a kid and something didn't go right at school, or I had a problem with a boy, or sat home instead of having a date to homecoming, my mom would give me a hug, tell me how smart and beautiful I was, immediately followed by "Stop feeling sorry for yourself, and figure out a way." I resented those comments at the time, thinking that she just didn't understand. Isn't that what all teenagers think? But so many nights since my life turned upside down, I have heard her voice, "Pick yourself up. Yes, you were dealt a bad hand, but you have to play it. You're stronger than you know. Figure something out." And so I have tried.

My mother was born in Chicago in 1923, and raised in several cities across the country, as my grandfather was a traveling advertising representative. She met my father in spring of 1945, just after World War II ended. They were engaged by July and married in November, just six months after meeting. Always one of the most conservative members of our family, Mom often warned first my sister and me, then our daughters, to protect virginity at all cost. Her oft-repeated phrase, through two generations, was "Why buy the cow when the milk is free?" One memorable Thanksgiving dinner, she was expressing this thought yet again to my daughters, teenagers at the time, and slipped into a story about taking a train to join my father - before they were married - at the base where he was stationed, much to her own mother's dismay. One of the girls questioned, "But Grandma, we thought you said we shouldn't do that?" To which my mother replied, with no hint of embarrassment, "Well, it was WARTIME!" That explained everything.

Always fit, Mom was on a never-ending mission to get my father to eat healthier and lose weight in the process. After he was diagnosed with heart disease, she bought every health craze cookbook on the market and starting experimenting with recipes, most of them awful. My dad would retaliate by snacking when she wasn't around. She would count out ten grapes to accompany his lunch; he would go to a Kiwanis meeting and have a couple of donuts. Try as she did, she never won that battle, but it wasn't for lack of perseverance.

My mother enjoyed golf, travel, bridge and the Arizona desert. Always one to give back, she spent many years volunteering for various organizations, from the PTA, to Girl Scouts, to the Florence Crittendon Association to the local library. She was an accomplished artist, and her oil paintings included still life, landscapes and portraits, both human and animal. She shared her beautiful tenor voice with a group called the Ring-a-Dings, as well as the Sweet Adeline's barbershop chorus. As a member of that group, she entertained at the Republican National Convention in Chicago in 1960. She also was a voracious reader and crossword puzzle aficionado. One of her greatest joys besides her family was her love of dogs. She loved them all, and they loved her right back.

When I had to sell my house and get rid of so many of my possessions, I discovered that many of the things I just could not part with had been passed down to me by my mother. When I was looking for a new home, it was mandatory to find one with a room big enough to house her dining room furniture. I just could not let it go. Her china, her crystal and her paintings surround me. I am also surrounded by her love. Her faith was shaky at best; she wasn't sure whether there was a life after death, but I know she is still looking out for me. I know she is still telling me to buck up, and "figure out a way." So I will, but I miss you Mom.

34 GRANDPARENT JOURNEY/JOY TIMES FIVE

A grandchild fills a space in your heart you never knew was empty.

Unknown

With my beautiful grandchildren, Spring 2018

J

anuary 13, 2010, September 10, 2010, December 10, 2012, February 13, 2015 and June 11, 2016 are five of the most important days of my life. Each one of them changed me for the better, as these are the birthdates of my five grandchildren. I was there for the birth of four of the last five, and on a plane cross-country within minutes of the birth of the first. Everybody thinks his or her grandchildren are the smartest, cutest, funniest, and most loving, and that's the way it should be, but mine really are. Allow me to introduce them:

Peyton, my firstborn is as smart as they come, loves reading, salad and broccoli. She thinks history is boring, but I am trying to change her mind. Her passion is gymnastics, and her best events are bars and floor. You might see her in the Olympics one day. She and I share a special bond, probably because she is the person that made me a grandmother.

Scott is my oldest grandson and shares my love for baseball. Since he was a toddler, we took him to games every year on his birthday, which he shares with Paul Goldschmidt, All Star first baseman for the Arizona Diamondbacks and Hall of Famer Randy Johnson. His heart (and mine) were recently broken when Paul was traded to the St. Louis Cardinals. His favorite subject is math and he's an incredible LEGO builder, taking only a few hours to put together a project of several hundred pieces. Then he takes it apart and builds something new from his imagination. His passion is all things NASA and space.

Charlotte is Scott's sister, but in no way does her big brother overshadow her. She is not afraid of anything, which she proved by asking to have a python draped around her neck at Scott's birthday party. She is compassionate and loving, and always tries to give her money away to friends, much to her mother's chagrin. She loves dancing and gymnastics. She also rarely wears pants or jeans, preferring a Princess costume if given the chance. Her passion is animals, and it wouldn't surprise me if she grew up to be a veterinarian.

Brendan is Peyton's little brother, and the comic relief in the family. He also is a dead ringer for my husband when he was a child. Five years younger than his big sister, he has in many ways forged his own way. He is equally comfortable drawing, playing with trucks or a play kitchen or putting a bucket on his head. He loves broccoli and Mac and cheese and swimming. His passion is all things Mickey Mouse or Paw Patrol.

Cameron is our baby and little sister to both Peyton and Brendan. Born only sixteen months after Brendan, she could pass for his twin. We all marveled at what a placid, easy baby she was, until she turned two. Not one to make things to easy for her parents, she almost overnight turned into someone who tested their patience at every turn. She loves spaghetti, annoying her brother, copying her sister, and giggling when she is in trouble. Her passion is getting into trouble.

My grandkids are so much more than that, of course. I believe they literally saved my life. After my husband died, I was in a downward spiral that seemed to have no end. I had not only lost my spouse, I lost my identity, my income, my possessions, my home, my very way of life. Each day was a struggle to get up in the morning, knowing that I had to face a myriad of decisions about taxes, credit card bills, social security, and earning a living. The one constant was that time spent with any one or all of my grandchildren, who put a smile on my face that all the problems of the world could not erase.

We had a tradition that I decided to continue even though I was now alone, and that was Pasta Wednesday. Pasta Wednesday in our home had actually begun a few years back in an unlikely place: a judge's chambers. During a break in a hearing, the judge asked my husband, "How long do you anticipate going this afternoon?"

"Not too much longer" came the reply.

"Good," said His Honor, "because tonight is Pasta Wednesday and I don't want to be late."

He went on to elaborate that Pasta Wednesday was a ritual he and his wife shared with their small grandchildren. Every Wednesday, the youngsters were picked up from school by the grandparents and brought to their house for dinner, crafts or an activity of some kind. Parents were intentionally and definitely not invited.

My husband thought this was a wonderful idea and came home that night   full of plans for our own Pasta Wednesdays. The only problem was we did not have any grandchildren yet. When we were finally blessed with two babies in the same year, plans for our own Pasta Wednesdays went into full effect. We began when our grandson turned one and our granddaughter was about twenty months. Those first evenings were mostly just dinner, stories and playtime. But as they grew older and more grandchildren joined the family, we progressed into cooking lessons, picnics in the park, holiday light tours, world trips (geography and history lessons), movie nights and special occasion parties. We adapted things a little bit over the years; for instance, even though the night was called Pasta Wednesday, it was not necessary to have pasta. My oldest grandson early on developed a dislike for anything related to spaghetti or noodles. What kid doesn't like spaghetti? So the title might have been a misnomer, but the kids all knew that "Pasta Wednesday" meant going to Grandma and Grandpa's house, and that's all that really mattered.

Halloween was always one of the biggest undertakings. The kids brought costumes, we had a Halloween-oriented dinner which included mummy wrapped hot dogs, spider sandwiches, and caterpillar grape sticks. We played some simple games, such as ghost toilet paper bowling, mummy wrapping and bobbing for apples. Then the kids worked their way through a balloon and crepe paper maze to the room where their goody bags were waiting

Yes, there's some prep work involved every week. Some weeks entail more than others, like the Halloween party. But truth be told, Pasta Wednesday has gotten me through many a dark day since the death of my husband. I had to cut it down to twice a month rather than every week as one adult and five little ones were a lot to handle while trying to sell my house and reorganize my life. Then it got changed again when two of the grandchildren moved to Indiana rather suddenly. But I still have it with the remaining three, and recreate it in some fashion when I visit Indiana. There is something about the laughter and unconditional love of those children that lets me forget about taxes and finances and selling and buying houses and growing a new business and all the rest of the reality of my life and worry about something much more important, like getting those crescent roll mummy hotdogs looking just right. It's the least I can do for the joy times five I get from them.

35 HEALING JOURNEY/NORWAY

It doesn't matter where you are. You are nowhere compared to where you can go.

Bob Proctor

F

or our forty-fifth wedding anniversary my husband and I had planned back-to-back bucket list cruises to Norway and Iceland. His untimely death occurred just about two months prior to departure and after the cruises had been paid for in full. We had not purchased travel insurance, as in my husband's words, "There is no need for it. I'm fine." It was another lesson learned, and a mistake I will not repeat.

My first thought was just to cancel and forfeit the money. But at the reception after my husband's funeral, my dear friend Candy sat next to me, held my hand and said,

"If you still feel like going, I will go with you so you don't have to be alone." Her husband Chris gave his blessing. What an incredible gift they both gave me.

Due to some connections I had with some ship personnel, I was able to get the non-refundable funds from the Iceland trip transferred to a future sailing, so I was able to cancel that portion without guilt and start to actually look forward to the Norway voyage. Coming on the heels of a disastrous auction experience and putting my house on the market, it was welcome relief.

The trip was magical. From the moment we arrived in Hamburg, our port of embarkation, to debarkation fourteen days later in Copenhagen, I felt like I was in a fairy tale. We met up with friends from Australia I had only known online and spent most of our time with them on and off the ship. Sara became a shoulder to cry on when I needed it, and her dear husband Frank kept reminding me of what was really important in my life. Frank quickly became the "husband" to three wives, his own, Candy and me.

Each port was more beautiful than the last. We walked in the rain in Bergen, took a breathtaking train ride in Flam, sailed through the Geiranger fjord, trekked up mountains, went to the top of the world at Nordkapp, visited quaint fishing villages, rode a sky lift, watched thousands of waterfalls, marveled at the Midnight Sun, ate fresh goat cheese, strawberries, salmon and king crab. The scenery was picture postcard perfect and the weather but for the one day in Bergen was outstanding.

But what I remember most was how kind everyone was to me. My husband and I had sailed on this ship many times in the past, and as it is a small vessel, had come to know many of the staff and crew. They all knew my situation, and everyone seemed to make it their personal mission to help me heal. The hotel director invited me for drinks, just to talk. My favorite waiter sought me out whenever I walked into a dining venue and hovered nearby to make sure I had everything I wanted or needed. The activities manager stuck close by, always ready with a joke or a smile. The cruise director joined me for meals or drinks on numerous occasions and even spent a day with us sightseeing. The Captain and his staff arranged for a burial at sea of some of my husband's ashes. He even invited Candy and me, along with the cruise director, for a private dinner in his stateroom. My favorite waiter volunteered to be our server that night.

My family is loving and patient and kind. I could not have survived without them. But they were grieving too, for different reasons and in a different way than I was. They could not always be there for me emotionally and I respect and understand that. My cruise ship friends became my other family for those magical two weeks and stepped into that void. Because of their constant and unconditional love, set against one of the most spectacular backdrops in the world, I was able to begin my healing process. The healing journey is a long and difficult one; one that I am still navigating. I have discovered that there is no timetable for when grief ends, if indeed it ever does. There have been and still are, many challenges ahead, but I know now that my healing began on a beautiful little cruise ship called the Azamara Journey in Norway. It will forever hold a very special place in my mending heart.

36 FRIENDSHIP JOURNEY/LIFELINES

"You raise me up to more than I can be."
Lyrics by Brendan Graham

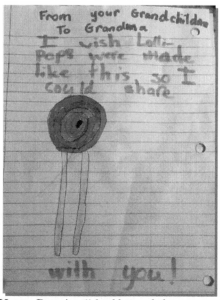

From "Happy Drawings" booklet made by my grandchildren

I woke up depressed and teary-eyed one morning after having just returned from a wonderful, exotic trip to the Middle East. I was feeling sorry for myself because it had ended. My house sold while I was gone, and I was overwhelmed by everything that had to be done in the next few weeks in order to vacate a home I didn't want to leave in the first place.

The seventh month mark since my husband's death had also just passed. Sometimes it felt like seven days; sometimes seven years. Because of circumstances I found myself in after his passing I had to make decisions and adjustments to my life and lifestyle that all experts say to put off for at least a year. The biggest of those decisions was selling my house, the place we had lived in for over thirty years, the house where we raised our family, used as a base for after school get-togethers and high school football rallies. It was the home from which both of our daughters were married, and it was the only home that our five grandchildren knew as "Grandma and Grandpa's house." Yet, it needed to be sold, and preferably as quickly as possible.

This major change, and other revelations left me traumatized on a regular basis in the months after my husband's death. I was not only grieving the life I knew that was suddenly yanked from me, I was faced with completely reprioritizing it with few resources. I discovered very quickly that I was simply not capable of navigating these new circumstances alone. Early on I was quite frankly paralyzed, and couldn't make a decision about what to wear or eat, much less something that was financially related. As the months went on, and the decisions became weightier, it seemed like every alternative was a bad one, and no decision an easy one.

Always an independent person, and always one who prided myself in my organizational skills, this was completely new territory for me. I needed help. And I needed friends. Thinking about all that as I woke up that morning made me dry my tears and realize this:

I was blessed, because the help and the friends came in many forms:

Family friends:

I believe I am the luckiest person on the planet, because my family really became my friends in ways I could never have imagined. My two daughters, Ginger and Kristy, took over every aspect of my everyday life those first horrible weeks. Grieving themselves, they put that aside to deal with funeral plans, death certificates, insurance, and a myriad of other mundane yet necessary chores. One took over the complete care and well being of my 93-year-old mother in-law, moving her from one care facility to another, taking her to the doctor, and coordinating her every need. The other took over getting our cabin rental-ready so I could derive some income from it to defray mortgage and other monthly expenses in the hopes of not having to liquidate that too. Both had the unwavering help and support of their husbands. Each of them invited me for dinner more than they needed to, and made sure I was rarely alone. My sons-in-law, Martin and Jim, took over the onerous task of cleaning out my husband's office, trying to determine what was important and should be kept and what could be tossed (no small feat because my husband could in no way be called a neatnik).

For comic relief and unconditional love, I had my five

grandchildren friends. Each played a role in trying to heal me, whether they knew it or not. The two oldest, Peyton and Scott, aged seven and six on the date of their grandfather's death, were old enough to comprehend what had happened. They were ever present at my side, giving me extra hugs, being extra good, and always watching me to see if I needed some more love from them. The middle child, Charlotte, age four, said to me so many times I lost count, "I'm so sorry you have to live alone now Grandma." What might have been heart wrenching was actually comforting; because she got it too and made me know she empathized. My 2-year-old grandson Brendan was my comic relief. He would ask where his grandpa was from time to time, but the next second he would run around the house with a bucket on his head, or want to play "tickle," one of his favorite games. Baby Cameron was the only one oblivious to everything at only ten months of age, but her smile, her laugh and her cuddles always made my heart melt. On one particular day when I was feeling pretty low, the grandkids must have been told. The three oldest ones spent their time after school making me a booklet of "Happy Drawings." I will cherish it always.

My only other close relative is my younger sister Dawn, who lived just a couple of streets from me. She rarely left my side those first awful days. Phone calls, dinner out or at her house, movies, a full day of lounging by the pool with adult beverages readily at hand on what would have been our 45th wedding anniversary, and which also happened to be the day I auctioned off a good percentage of my belongings, were all gestures that kept me sane.

Professional friends:

I am lucky to have a good medical doctor. She was in fact a high school classmate of one of my daughters. That may be a little strange, but since I have known her so long, I am comfortable with her. She listened to me for hours on various visits; prescribed some much need sleep and stress aids and recommended counseling.

I did try professional counseling with two different providers, but found it just did not help me much. I resisted group counseling for a long time, but finally decided to give it a try. For me, it ended up being a godsend. I found the members of my group to be empathetic, understanding and non-judgmental. On more than one occasion, they lifted me up and made me feel not so alone. The group became a lifeline, and I'm glad I kept trying until I found something that worked for me.

Faced with selling my house, I turned to a long time realtor friend. He was honest and caring, and talked me down from hysteria several times when I was impatient, frustrated and scared that I wouldn't get enough out of the house for my needs. It took four months, one rejected offer and two contracts, but we finally got it done.

My financial advisor literally became like another son to me. He exuded such calm whenever I panicked (which was often), always told me everything was going to be all right, and that he would make sure my assets were protected. I don't know if I valued him more for his financial advice or for his caring attitude. Either way, I am lucky to have him.

Personal friends:

I discovered early on in this process that I did not have as many as I thought I did. I also discovered that many that I thought were friends disappeared from my life once my husband died. But that's okay, because the ones I did have were the gold standard.

There was Claudia, a widow herself, who came to the hospital to be with me as soon as we knew my husband had died, just as the sun was coming up. She stayed with me that entire day, right beside me on the couch. Her close physical presence felt like a warm blanket on a cold day.

There were Diana and Dennis who came in from California to be with me for the funeral, do one of the eulogies, and who cooked, cleaned, ran errands and generally kept me together.

There was my long time friend Mark from Tennessee who dropped everything and stayed by my side for almost an entire week, just being. He is one of the few people I know I can call at any time for any reason for a sympathetic ear and unconditional love. There was his wife Tina, who unselfishly gave her blessing for him to come, even though his job keeps him on the road much of the year and she had to sacrifice a rare week at home with him.

There was Mindy, my sister from another mother, who usually knew what I was thinking before I did. She stayed in constant touch through phone calls and texts to make sure I was doing okay.

There was my thirty year plus friend Candy, who in the midst of a move herself, dropped everything to go on a trip my husband and I had planned for our 45th wedding anniversary, so I wouldn't have to be alone. Her husband Chris gave his unconditional blessing. She also has been known to come over at a moment's notice to cry with me over a glass of wine or three.

There was Alice, my phone and messaging friend who always told me to "face forward."

There were my longtime friends from the Oak Ridge Boys and

their organization, former and present: Duane, Joe, Richard, William Lee, Mark, Donna, Rex, Scotty, Ron, Jeff, Roger, Zeke, Darrick, Jon, Kathy, Mike, Dave, Skip, Chris, Paul, Jamie, Gaylea, Jen, Timmer and others who called, texted, emailed, sent flowers, listened, checked on me and did all they could to keep my spirits up.

There was my cruise director and recording artist friend Eric, who became the person with sage advice, no judgments, and who let me wallow in self-pity for only so long. He always managed to lift my spirits and make me feel loved. He listened to my fears, soothed my tears and calmed my soul. Most of the time he's many time zones away, yet he was and is *always* there.

Furry friends:

I have a ten year old dog named Gracie, who is nuts. She is an Australian Cattle dog mix, and still thinks she is a puppy. She had a "brother" named Reagan, who disliked her intensely and who died at the ripe old age of seventeen years, just a month before my husband. She had some trouble adjusting to that. When my husband died, although he was never her biggest fan either, she certainly felt his loss. Since that time, she has rarely left my side during the day, and in the evenings rests her head on my knee or lays on my feet. Every. Single. Night.

So as the worst year of my life finally, mercifully approached its end, I counted my blessings. They were in the form of the laughter of children, the love of a wonderful family, the wisdom of some great professionals, the gift of beautiful, loving friends, and the earnest brown eyes of a crazy dog. How lucky could a girl get?

37 GRIEF JOURNEY/ONE YEAR MARK

Life takes its own turns, makes its own demands, writes its own story, and along the way we start to realize we are not the author.

George W. Bush

Festival of Light ceremony in Thailand

A s the first anniversary of my husband's death approached, I began to reflect on how my life had changed forever. Twelve months. Fifty-two weeks. Three hundred sixty-five days. Five hundred twenty-five thousand, six hundred minutes. Thirty-one million three hundred fifty-six thousand seconds. Sometimes it seemed like it had gone by in a blink of the eye. Other times I relived every excruciating second.

My family and I had endured every one of the "firsts": Easter, Mothers' Day, our wedding anniversary, Fathers' Day, birthdays (ours and his), Thanksgiving, Christmas, and Valentine's Day. Some were easier than others, but all had an extra guest at the table, for the spirit of my husband was ever present. It was something that was rarely spoken about, but yet everyone felt.

The year had been full of upheaval. I sold a house and bought another. I shed myself of possessions acquired over a lifetime, many of them sentimental treasures. I dealt with robo calls to banks and mortgage lenders, accountants, lawyers and creditors. I took out the trash, changed light bulbs, assembled furniture and repaired a toilet, all things my husband would have done. I had to go back to work when all my friends were retiring, so I bought a travel business and dealt with all the legalities involved without my attorney husband's advice. I felt sorry for myself. I screamed when no one could hear me and cried endless tears. I questioned my faith. I felt adrift, like a ship without a sail, tossing about in an angry sea. I endured countless sleepless nights worrying about the future. I tested friendships. I leaned on people when I could not stand up by myself. I listened to people tell me it was time to move on, and tried not to be angry with them because they just didn't understand. No one could understand unless they were me.

Yet I was so very grateful to those who held my hand, were on the receiving end of plaintive phone calls and emails and texts, encouraged me, and hugged me. They were just there. They might not have fully understood the depths of my despair, but they loved me through it.

And so the first year was over. I survived, and if that was my only accomplishment, I was proud of it. There were times when even survival itself was in jeopardy. Five little people, their parents and a few dear souls wouldn't allow me to give up. They literally saved my life by their constant love and support and I am forever grateful.

On a trip to Southeast Asia I participated in the re-enactment of a Thai ritual called Loy Krathong, or the Festival of Light. The festival is celebrated nationwide in Thailand in November by releasing lotus shaped baskets, decorated with candles and flowers into the rivers. The release symbolizes letting go of all negativity and making a wish for the future. I found it prophetic that the re-enactment I participated in came just before the first anniversary of my husband's death. Two people who are very dear to me reminded me independently within days of each other that we have a choice as to how we react to adversity. They were right, although that is sometimes hard to believe when you are in the midst of hell. But as I released my flower into the water, I chose to say goodbye to so many negative thoughts that had been consuming me the past year.

I chose to let go of all the anger and bitterness. It was time, for I finally realized that holding on to all of that was accomplishing nothing and was a waste of my energy. As I watched the flower float along the pond, its candle flickering in the gentle night breeze, I felt a peace come over me that I hadn't felt in twelve months. I won't pretend that I was healed, nor was I foolish enough to think that with this first year over, all troubles would magically disappear. I was still going to be alone for dinner every night, I was still going to have to take out the trash and do home repairs as best I could, I was still going to cry (usually at the most unexpected times), and I was still going to face difficult challenges. My husband was gone and he was never coming back. My old life, one I loved, was over. That was the hard, terrible truth. I had a new life now and I alone had to define it. I wasn't going to pretend it would be easy. But I had survived year one. My goal for year two was to choose to live.

38 BITTERSWEET JOURNEY/LONG DISTANCE GRANDMA

Together forever, never apart. Sometimes in distance, but never in heart.

Anonymous

s

Scott and Charlotte, the Indiana grandkids

O n top of everything else I dealt with in the first year of widowhood, two-fifths of my world left me. That's equivalent to the landmasses of Russia, China, the United States, Canada, Brazil and Australia combined being erased from the earth. That's a lot, and it left a huge hole in my heart. It was another adjustment I didn't want to make, just a year after becoming a widow. I hadn't fully acclimated to that change yet; now I was asked to absorb this one.

The reason for their departure was a good one; my daughter received a huge promotion, but it meant relocating from the desert southwest to the midwest. She still works for the same newspaper entity, so there is every possibility that a transfer back HOME remains on the table. But for now, my two young grandchildren have joined their parents in a place that might as well be the moon.

Yes, airplanes fly. Yes, we are lucky to have Skype, Facetime, Messenger and all those great techie things that bring us closer together. Yes, this was a wonderful opportunity for my daughter, and I am so proud of her I could burst. But why does my heart feel so empty? It is not the same. I can no longer go to Little League games on Saturdays, or dance recitals or gymnastics meets. I can no longer have them overnight, just because, or babysit when their Mom and Dad go out for dinner. And they can't come to Pasta Wednesday. There are so many negatives.

I made my first trip to Indiana to visit about three months after the big move, on the occasion of my grandson's eighth birthday. First stop, directly from the airport was my granddaughter's gymnastics practice. The way her face lit up and she ran to me with arms outstretched when she saw me enter the gym almost made their move worth it. Maybe the heart does grow fonder with absence?

My grandson's birthday party was a cacophony of noise from a dozen or more eight year olds, running all over the house and squealing at the menagerie of animals that had also been invited as part of the entertainment. Pictures of me with a python around my neck will no doubt be part of family lore for years to come.

We baked cookies, and made back to school candy treats. We had a sleepover in the basement, just the three of us. I picked them up from school and read them bedtime stories. We went to a movie and out to eat. We did all the normal things we had done for years in Arizona, only this time is was done 1700 miles further east. I did my best to convince myself that not much had changed; I could still visit them, and they could come back to Arizona to see the family, and we were all still able to enjoy each other and our traditions. Seventeen hundred miles is a far cry from less than three, but for now we all needed to get used to it.

Maybe someday my daughter will get transferred back home, but until then, I have unwillingly joined the ranks of a long distance Grandma. I need to figure out how to make the best of it.

39 EQUILIBRIUM JOURNEY/THE TRAIN OF LIFE

Instead of saying "I'm damaged, I'm broken, I have trust issues" say "I'm healing, I'm rediscovering myself, I'm starting over."

Horacio Jones

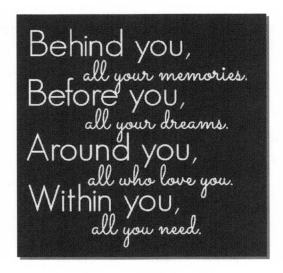

A s I wrote the last chapter of this book, I was also approaching my 70th birthday. And as I reflected back on all the joys and sorrows of the past sixty-nine years, I realized that the former have far outweighed the latter. I was blessed with a happy, no, idyllic childhood. I never wanted for anything, and most of all I had parents who loved me unconditionally; a sister who annoyed me at times, but became a rock for me to lean on and a trusted friend. I spent most of my adult years in a stable marriage, raising two beautiful daughters who have gifted me with the five amazing grandchildren that are the joys of my life.

Due to my job as a travel advisor, I have been lucky enough to travel all over the world. I've been to fifty-five countries and left my heart in many places. I've left it in vineyards and serene villages, in bustling cities and quiet canals. I've river rafted in the New Zealand Alps, fallen off a bike into a swamp in Vietnam, ridden a camel in Jordan, walked the beaches of Normandy, and the paths of the Great Wall of China, Petra and Old Havana. I've tasted haggis in Scotland, sushi in Japan, and enjoyed brunch in Dubai at the tallest building in the world. I've shopped for silk in Thailand, leather in Italy and cheese in France. I've visited churches and temples and mosques. And I've found peace on the deck of a beloved cruise ship, my safe haven, the Azamara Journey. I've willingly scattered my soul in so many locations. Each place has been a new learning experience and a fresh story to tell. And in dark times, the memory of each has given me solace.

In contrast, the sorrows of my life have been fewer in number, but crushing in their enormity. My nature has always been to look at things as the "worse case scenario," or the "glass half empty." That way, when things inevitably turned out better than I anticipated, I was able to take on life's challenges with aplomb and energy. It's a character flaw I know, and one I am determined to change.

However, the events of the past few years made all my worse case scenarios seem even more terrible than even I had imagined them to be. Blow after blow took its toll, and finding my equilibrium was harder than I ever imagined. But I felt like I was making progress. I bought a new home that I was enjoying very much, I was still able to travel some, I found a grief therapy group that was helpful, and I truly felt like I was "moving on." I had released that lotus flower into the water, letting go of my anger and feeling peace for the first time in a very long time. But the peace was not to last long. The roller coaster ride of grief was about to take another enormous plummet.

The one-year mark of my husband's death almost exactly coincided with the end of that wonderful cruise to Southeast Asia with my younger daughter. While I know I should have focused on the great time we had and the memories we made, my immediate emotion was sadness because of having to come home from my safe haven on that ship to my reality, which was not such a happy place. Add jet lag, and it was not pretty.

A day after returning home, my older daughter broke the news that she had accepted the huge promotion that would take her family to Indiana, in less than a month. I was very proud of her, yet all I could think of was my loss. My grandchildren were going to move half a country away and I was no longer going to be a part of their daily lives. The pain was deep and consuming.

The actual day of the first anniversary (and why is the term "anniversary" used for such a milestone anyway?) was more difficult for me than I thought it would be. I couldn't help compare what my life was like a year ago to what it was now, so full of uncertainty. I did my best not to feel sorry for myself anymore, but sometimes those feelings got the best of me.

To top it all off, I got a whopping tax bill for the second year in a row, in the five figures, for a second year in a row. That meant that almost half of the total life insurance I received had been paid to the U.S. government. This harsh reality indicated I now had to face selling my beloved cabin in northern Arizona, a place I had hoped to leave to my children. Another loss loomed. In addition, I was trying to get a new travel agency business off the ground, which takes time and energy on a daily basis that I just did not always have.

All of this met in a perfect storm as that April progressed. I tried very hard to maintain my equilibrium, but each crushing blow right on top of one another made it very difficult. I was tired. Tired of all the setbacks, tired of worrying about the future, tired of being alone to make all these decisions, small and large, every second of every day. And this was only the end of year one. I knew I had the rest of my life to face these challenges. I was tired physically (I never slept well anymore), and tired emotionally. "Choosing to live" as I had promised myself to do, was easier said than done.

I drove to my cabin one weekend to get away, and as the winding road became mountainous the further north I drove, I couldn't help but wonder if the pain could just be stopped by accelerating and aiming the car over one of the steep cliffs. I contemplated this possibility for miles. Two things stopped me from actually doing it: cowardice in the likelihood I wouldn't succeed in taking my life and end up crippled or burned or both instead, and the faces of my grandchildren flashing before me. They didn't deserve to live with that burden.

It was with this pity party frame of mind that I reached out to a few friends. A couple of them just let me cry. There was nothing they could do but listen, but it helped. Another tried to recalculate my taxes to see if there might have been a mistake. There wasn't, but the effort was appreciated. And then there was my friend Eric, who kicked my ass. He told me in no uncertain terms that despite everything, I had much to be thankful for: a home, food on the table, a loving family, grandchildren who looked up to me, people who cared about me. And what was my reaction? To lash out, because although I knew in my heart the ass-kicking was warranted, I preferred to feel sorry for myself. It was easier to be miserable than to find the courage to move forward. Only when he suggested that it was time for him to "step back" did I start to come to my senses, for I couldn't bear to lose his friendship.

While wallowing in my misery, I decided to conduct an experiment. I instituted a self-imposed ban on all emailing, texting, messaging, commenting and posts on social media for ten days. I wanted to see if anybody even noticed, if anybody reached out, if anybody really cared like I was assured they did. As was my nature, I assumed I would hear from few people, if any. After all I reasoned, they all had their own lives to live, they were tired of my problems, it's been a year, I should be over this, and on and on. So I kept a daily log. On day one, I got a request for a favor. On the morning of day two, there was another one. That afternoon, however, I received an email from my sister with a picture of her beautiful lilac tree. Along with Lillie's of the Valley, lilacs were my grandmother's favorite flower. I adored my grandmother and fondly remember looking forward to watching her lilac bush bloom every spring. The photo reminded me of her and her unconditional love, which in turn reminded me of my grandkids and how precious they were to me. That simple email also reminded me that like my grandmother before me, I have little people who loved me and looked up to me. I felt a sliver of equilibrium returning.

That same night I received a video entitled "The Train of Life" from the very person who had kicked my fanny and suggested it was time to step away from me, my friend Eric. The video was about how we board our train as infants, and ride along with our parents. We meet people along the way, some more important than others. At some point our parents leave the train, and we are left to travel alone. More people will get on and off as the train travels along. What we don't know is when it will be our turn to get off, so we must make the most of the ride and leave happy, lasting memories for the ones left behind when we leave. I watched the video several times over, with tears in my eyes, for instead of quitting on me, Eric was showing love and concern for me. I felt God was sending me a message of encouragement, and an angel to deliver it. And I felt peace. A few days later there was another message from Eric, just checking on me and hoping that things were looking up. I will never be able to express how his outreach at such a low time gave me the courage to go on. From the moment my husband died, this man has been my rock and my angel. I can talk to him when I can talk to no one else. He has been a constant in an otherwise turbulent storm, someone who quite literally saved my life. I always thought my husband and I were put in his path to help him record a CD in Nashville; I know now God used that as a catalyst so he could be there for me in my darkest hours. Although our relationship is strictly platonic and always will be, I could not ask for a better confidant and friend.

In the days that followed I received more unsolicited messages from close friends, both old and new. Most of them were just simple questions inquiring about my well-being. But I took each one of them as a sign that I was not forgotten, and that people actually did care. It's something that I suppose everyone needs to be assured of from time to time, but it is especially true for those of us who are alone.

Those messages were a turning point for me. I stopped looking at the negatives and looked at the positives first for a change. I stopped feeling sorry for myself. And it has made all the difference. I have no idea what the next chapter of my life will bring, but I believe with all my heart that the picture in the Prologue is a sunrise rather than a sunset, and more importantly, it is within my power to make it just that.

EPILOGUE: THERE'S A PONY IN HERE SOMEWHERE

A s I was watching the extensive coverage of the 60th anniversary of the D-Day landings in 2004 a crawl headline came across the screen: "Family gathering as Reagan's condition worsens." This was not unexpected, as former President Reagan was ninety-three years old and had been ravaged by Alzheimer's Disease for ten years. But it hit me hard. Ronald Reagan had been the only President I had really campaigned for, and I thought he was indestructible.

Within a few short hours, however, the news came that he had died. And thus began a weeklong series of ceremonies to honor him and ultimately lay him to rest. Virtually all other programming was pre-empted by images of brass bands, a caisson, a rider less horse, the casket lying in state, his widow Nancy on the arm of her military escort, and cross country plane rides. The air was filled with the strains of "Hail to the Chief" and several twenty-one gun salutes. Presidents and world leaders paid eloquent tribute; his children, once estranged, now eulogized him. At every ceremony, thousands waited in line to pay their respects. The number of

Americans who came out to honor him stunned even his closest family members and supporters.

Pundits spent hours and days dissecting his administration and his legacy. Over and over again they pointed to his part in ending the Cold War without firing a shot, his tax cuts, his belief that every person on earth longed to be free, and that America was the greatest country on earth; a shining City on a Hill. They lauded him for bringing hope and pride back to this country. They discussed his communication skills, that he would be forever known as the Great Communicator. But there was one brief interview that summed him and his philosophy up in a short story. He told an aide after a long, tedious meeting of world leaders that seemed to accomplish little; "There's a pony in there somewhere." Asked to explain, President Reagan told a story: On Christmas morning a small boy went to the tree to find his presents. Instead of gaily wrapped gifts, all he found was a huge pile of manure. Digging through it with all his might, he was heard to exclaim, "There's a pony in here somewhere!"

Those six words I believe sum up the legacy of President Reagan. Through all the manure, he always looked for the pony, and usually found it. He taught me the same thing. No matter how much manure is thrown at me (and there has been a lot in the last few years), I'm going to keep on looking for those ponies.

ABOUT THE AUTHOR

Holly Richardson was born to Greatest Generation parents, is a child of the fifties, attended college in the turbulent sixties, came of age in the seventies, raised children in the eighties and nineties, and was widowed at the age of 68. She is truly a Baby Boomer. She has published articles on subjects from baseball to travel to country music stars, maintains a blog on her life experiences (www.journeysofaboomer.com) and has traveled extensively all over the world, due to many years in the travel industry. Currently she is the owner of Journeys of Dreams, a full service agency. (www.journeysofdreams.com) She has two married daughters and five grandchildren and lives in Scottsdale, Arizona with her dog Gracie. This is her first book.

Made in the USA
Monee, IL
25 August 2019